D1549039

I

2

Reviewed by the
Parent-Teacher Advisory Board

Developmental Overview by Nancy Richard

becker & mayer!
BOOKS

A FIRESIDE BOOK
Published by Simon & Schuster

JENNIFER RICHARD JACOBSON
AND DOTTIE RAYMER

How Is My *Fourth Grader* Doing in School?

WHAT TO EXPECT AND HOW TO HELP

Fireside
Rockefeller Center
1230 Avenue of the Americas
New York, NY 10020

becker & mayer!
BOOKS

Produced by becker&mayer!
www.beckermayer.com

BOOK DESIGNED BY BARBARA MARKS

Assessment booklet designed by Heidi Baughman
Interior illustrations by Cary Pillo, Matt Hutnak, and Dan Minnick
becker&mayer! art director: Simon Sung
becker&mayer! editor: Jennifer Worick

Manufactured in the United States of America

1 3 5 7 9 10 8 6 4 2

Library of Congress Cataloging-in-Publication Data
Jacobson, Jennifer, date.
How is my fourth grader doing in school? : what to expect and how to help /
by Jennifer Richard Jacobson and Dottie Raymer ; developmental overview by Nancy Richard.
p.   cm.
"Becker & Mayer! books."
Includes index.
1. Fourth grade (Education)—United States.   2. Education, Primary—Parent participation—United
States.   3. Parent-teacher relationships—United States.   4. Language arts (Primary)—United States.
5. Mathematics—Study and teaching (Primary)—United States.   I. Title.   II. Raymer, Dottie.
LB1571 4th.J33   2000
372.24'1—dc21   98-39750
CIP

ISBN 0-684-85719-7

Acknowledgments

We would like to give special thanks to Nancy Richard, who wrote the Developmental Overview for this book. Nancy has been a student of child development, school readiness, and effective classroom practices for the past thirty years. She has worked with thousands of teachers and parents throughout the country to promote classrooms that are educationally successful as well as responsive to the developmental needs of children. She has served on the national lecture staff of the Gesell Institute of Human Development and has been a consulting teacher for the Northeast Foundation for Children. She co-authored the book *One Piece of the Puzzle: A School Readiness Manual.*

In addition, we would like to thank the members of our Parent Teacher Advisory Board who volunteered countless hours to reading and critiquing the books in this series. They have graciously shared their educational knowledge and insight. Their wisdom, gathered through years of working with children in classrooms, has enriched these books tremendously. Their guidance has been invaluable. Members of the Parent Teacher Advisory Board are as follows:

Jim Grant, a former teacher and principal, is an internationally known consultant and one of America's most passionate advocates for children. He is the founder of the Society for Developmental Education, the nation's primary provider of staff development training for elementary teachers. He is also founder and co-executive director of the National Alliance of Multiage Educators. The author of dozens of professional articles and educational materials, his books *"I Hate School!" Some Common-Sense Answers for Educators & Parents Who Want to Know Why and What to Do About It, Retention and Its Prevention,* and *A Common-Sense Guide to Multiage Practices* are recognized resources for teachers, parents, and administrators.

Mary Mercer Krogness, a public school teacher for over thirty years, is the recipient of the Martha Holden Jennings Master Teacher Award, the highest recognition the foundation bestows on a classroom teacher in Cleveland, Ohio. She has taught grades k–8 in both urban and suburban schools and is currently a language arts consultant for five school systems, an educational speaker, and an author. In addition to award-winning articles, Mary is the author of *Just Teach Me, Mrs. K: Talking, Reading, and Writing with Resistant Adolescent Learners,* and is the writer/producer of an award-winning, nationally disseminated **PBS** television series, *Tyger, Tyger, Burning Bright,* a creative writing program for elementary age students.

Connie Plantz, an elementary school teacher for over twenty years, has had extensive experience with students of economic, academic, and cultural diversity. In addition to being a classroom teacher, she has held the titles of grade level leader, reading specialist, teacher of gifted and talented students, and chairperson of the Multicultural Committee. She has developed curricula and acted as an educational consultant for homeschoolers and educational publishing companies, and has taught graduate courses in reading and teacher education at National University. Connie also reviews children's literature and is the author of fiction and nonfiction, including *Pacific Rim,* for middle grade readers.

Robert (Chip) Wood is the co-founder of the Northeast Foundation for Children, a nonprofit educational foundation whose mission is the improvement of education in elementary and middle schools. The foundation provides training, consultation, and professional development opportunities for teachers and administrators. It also operates a k–8 laboratory school for children and publishes articles and books (by teachers) for educators and parents. Chip has served NEFC as a classroom teacher, consultant, and executive director. He is the author of many professional articles and the book, *Yardsticks: Children in the Classroom, Ages 4–14,* and co-author of *A Notebook for Teachers: Making Changes in the Elementary Curriculum.*

It takes many people to create a book. We would like to thank the talented staff at becker&mayer who produced this book, especially Jim Becker, who offered this idea; Andy Mayer, who has followed it through; Jennifer Worick, who graciously navigated this book through all channels; Simon Sung, who coordinated art; Heidi Baughman, who designed the assessment booklet; Jennifer Doyle, who worked with panel members; Matt Hutnak, who drew computer sketches; and Kelly Skudlarick, who worked on the original proposal.

We would also like to acknowledge the members of the Simon & Schuster publishing group, particularly Trish Todd, who has shared our vision and commitment to this series; Cherise Grant, who has been engaged in all aspects of production; Barbara Marks, who designed the book; Toni Rachiele, production editor; and Marcela Landres, who did a little bit of everything.

And finally we would like to thank the countless teachers, parents, and children who have offered their knowledge, anecdotes, insights, artwork, and advice. We hope you recognize your contributions on these pages.

Contents

How is my Fourth Grader Doing in School?

Introduction

Welcome to fourth grade. Your child is one of the big kids now. How does it feel?

Your answer might depend upon how your school system is set up. If your fourth grader still has a year or two to go in elementary school, you may be feeling fairly comfortable. If, on the other hand, your child is moving on to the middle school next year, you may be feeling apprehensive. Will your child be ready for the academic and emotional demands? You wonder how your child is *really* doing.

For your child, too, life is different. Academics are getting tougher. Expectations are more rigorous. The schedule is jam-packed. Children who have glided through school up until now may run into unexpected difficulties. A good reader becomes reluctant. A fine math student dissolves into tears over a sheet of division problems. Yes, things have definitely changed.

What's a parent to do? Luckily, you can be the one thing that hasn't changed in your child's academic life. Your involvement in your child's education this year is more important than ever. Research has shown that parent participation in a child's education is the leading factor in academic success. Children from all socioeconomic backgrounds are happier, more motivated, and get better grades when their parents take an active role in their learning. Contrary to popular belief, or even your own instincts, this involvement becomes even more important as your child gets older. You know your child better than anyone else. You know that she likes to read lying upside down on her bed. You know that she can do a math problem twice as fast if she narrates her way through it. You know what interests her, what motivates her, and how she has always learned best. You were your child's first teacher. Even as she moves out into the world of friends and sports and school activities, you are still her most important teacher.

That's all very well, you might say, but where can we find the time? Middle graders are busy people. Lessons and sports events and all sorts of social events with very important friends leave little time for homework, let alone extra study time. Being involved in your child's learning, however, need not take extra time. And it certainly *should not* take the form of "extra study time." All you really have to do is use the time that you already have—those five minutes on the way to the soccer field, that restless time just before dinner—as "teachable moments," informal, creative moments that can help your child grow and flourish. As you begin to notice these moments and the opportunities they provide, you will find that your time with your child feels not busier, but more connected and high-spirited.

This book is intended to help you use those precious moments to their fullest extent. It comes with an observational assessment that will help you determine what in the traditional fourth grade curriculum your child knows and what might be helpful to introduce to her next. This assessment is not a standardized test. It is not an IQ test. In this assessment, you will not find any quantifiable scores or percentiles. Instead, you will find ways for you to observe how your child approaches learning. If you watch carefully, you might find the results surprising.

As with all the books in this series, the learning activities in *How Is My Fourth Grader Doing in School?* cover the broad strokes of the fourth grade reading, writing, and math curriculum. Science, social studies, the arts, and physical education are not covered because the content in these subjects varies from school to school and cannot be presented accurately. Nevertheless, they are essential to a sound education, and your child needs to know that you value these subjects as well. Find out what your child is studying in these areas and see if there is a way you can contribute. Explore new knowledge in science and social studies, go to museums, attend concerts and plays. Discover how rewarding learning with your child can be.

Developmental Overview

by Nancy Richard

All children are individuals. They have their own personalities and grow at different rates. They have different genes and are influenced by different environments. Yet children at the same developmental stage are surprisingly alike. This is true of almost every stage and grade except fourth grade, when nature highlights the individuality of children, emphasizing their personal interests, talents, and learning styles. Fourth grade, perhaps more than any other, might give you a peek at the potential and future direction of your child. Here are some of the traits you might see in your child.

From Fear to Competence

When teachers are asked about the traits of fourth graders, the first trait mentioned is often their need for perfection and their fear of looking bad. Because fourth graders want to be considered competent by their teacher, but especially by their classmates, they usually won't take risks unless a climate of mutual respect and caring has been established in the classroom. Coupled with this need to look good is a competitiveness that can get out of hand inside the classroom as well as outside if it isn't checked. Children should be encouraged to compete against themselves and not with each other. In some fourth grade classrooms where being kind and respectful is a priority, teachers report that children encourage and support each other, even cheer each other on.

Fear of not being competent also shows up in the introduction of new material or skills. Nine-to-ten-year-olds are often reluctant to try anything new, fearing they won't be able to do it. However, once this reluctance is overridden, and once they have the skills, they will work tirelessly on perfecting them. Then, feeling confident and competent, they will branch out in all directions, probing into the depths of material, delightedly experimenting and creating.

Probing Minds

If you listen carefully to the language of children, you can get a real sense of how they think. If you listen to almost any discussion on any subject with fourth graders, you will hear them express a version of "and then what—and then what?" Most fourth graders want to think in depth. They would rather take one subject and explore it thoroughly than cover many subjects superficially.

For this reason, some fourth grade teachers will take a thematic approach, in which perhaps three or more themes are explored for several weeks to several months. Some examples might be the constellations, community conservation, or state history. There are endless possibilities for themes, and teachers choose them to incorporate the greatest number of appropriate skills. The children then study the chosen theme through field trips, reading, and research. They plan their projects and how they will present them, whether through art, writing, drama, or maybe by needlework or construction of a model.

This method meets many of the needs of the nine-to-ten-year-old for in-depth study. Moreover, it provides for another characteristic seen in many nine-to-ten-year-old children: their almost fanatic affinity for detail.

Attention to Detail

This affinity for detail often leads fourth grade teachers to introduce their children to the tools of research. The whole class might be researching one subject, but more often each child might be researching a different subject, all learning to use the same research tools. Children at this stage are ripe for extended uses of the dictionary, encyclopedia, and thesaurus. The thesaurus captivates many. Atlases are another favorite.

The love of detail, which is fairly general in fourth graders, will show itself in the individual interests and talents of children. Some children want to embellish their handwriting and aspire to the skill of calligraphy. Others are attracted to drafting, with its precision and beautiful tools. Children who are mechanical might draw machines with intricate detail.

Fourth graders' interest in detail often shows up in their artwork. A drawing of a tree, for instance, might contain spiders, spiderwebs, butterflies, and cocoons. The bark as well as the leaves and fruit might be elaborately defined. Many children who are artistically inclined will use sketching or shading techniques, and they often like to use pencil, pencil crayons, or pen, which all show detail better than markers or crayons. They love using new media such as Sharpie pens that allow them to make very intricate strokes. Craypas, another favorite, allow them to do blending and to copy the style of the French impressionists. New media also extend the number of possibilities for becoming competent.

Visual Strength

Most fourth grade children have a heightened visual sense. These children are readily drawn to pictures, diagrams, and maps in all areas of study. Introducing them to a subject through a visual medium often cuts down on their beginning anxiety.

For example, a resourceful fourth grade teacher uses the visual strength and love of detail of the fourth grader to teach writing. The children in her class choose a picture they like from a picture book. They discuss such details as perspective, distance, and proportion. They talk about style and the kinds of media the artist used. Through this process, the children begin to internalize the criteria for good art. They then re-create a portion of the picture or the whole picture. Later, they will describe the picture using nouns, verbs, and adjectives. They will develop topic sentences and main ideas, and eventually they will write an original story from all of their detailed information.

Fourth graders are ripe for introduction to fine art—through a museum, if one is available, or through books if not. The different styles and techniques of different artists fascinate them. There is also an interest in and an aptitude for handiwork with both girls and boys in the fourth grade. Many are drawn to quilt making, embroidery, weaving, or even simple sewing techniques. If the children are given the time to practice and to become proficient, they will choose these activities over and over again.

Time, Independence, and Choice

Because fourth graders are very detail-oriented and because they are perfectionists, they require a good deal of time to do their work. However, a common fourth grade problem is lack of time. Often scheduling and the requirements of the fourth grade curriculum demand that work be hurried, which ultimately frustrates the children. If they're reading or being read to, they don't want to stop or go on to something else before they are satisfied. In their writing, also, they need lots of time: time to get started, time to get absorbed in the writing, time to try out ideas.

The sheer number of things the fourth grader wants to do in a day can create a problem with time. She wants to go to Girl Scouts, take flute lessons, play soccer, and play with her friends as well as go to school, do homework, and watch her favorite shows on television.

Most fourth graders like to do things their own way. They like to plan and to think things through to have an idea of what their finished project will be like. They want to help plan the school day and their time at home. They want choices built into their lives: a choice of what they'll work on in school; a choice of what they'll do after school; a choice of organized activity or free play. However, because there are so many things that they want to accomplish, fourth graders often have difficulty with time management and organizational skills. They need help structuring both their time and their activity.

Schoolwork

Fourth graders learn from the specific to the general. For example, learning the skills involved with the use of the protractor and compass lead to the making of pie graphs and exploration of design. Like their younger counterparts from kindergarten through third grade, they learn best through the handling of materials and tools: from the concrete to the abstract.

Most fourth graders like to write and want the feedback that will help them improve both the vitality and voice of their writing and the appearance of their work. But they need to be given the time to write, to edit, and even to embellish their work a bit to satisfy their need for a good product. Editing still is not easy for them, although it is much easier for them to delete material than it was in third grade. They are more willing to edit if they can work on short pieces or those that are less complicated.

In their writing they now display the correct use of the comma, dash, apostrophe, and italics. They especially like quotation marks. Their choice of words usually meets the standards of good grammar. Many know the basic conventions of writing letters and like to write to friends or pen pals. Some children like to write business letters to order things from catalogs. Others send away for things they can get for free. More than one fourth grade child has done this as a hobby.

In math, fourth graders like to analyze the processes involved both in doing calculations and in solving problems. They especially want to analyze their mistakes. Since ways of finding solutions will be different for different children, it is important that your child understand his own processes. Ask him to show you how he figured out a problem. Respect the fact that he might think about the problem differently from you and work it out in a different way. In fact, encourage him to figure problems out in different ways. Most children of this stage appreciate the fact that there are a lot of ways of doing things.

This year the children will be mastering the times tables that were started in third grade. They will be working on fractions and decimals; measurement, percentages, and word problems; and most will be doing division using one-digit divisors. An aspect of division that is apt to give fourth graders a problem is the *remainder*. It's hard for them to understand that all things in math don't come out equal.

Fourth graders need lots of math practice. They are now able to memorize the math facts they need for quick calculation: addition and subtraction combinations; the times tables; and common measurement standards, such as the number of feet in a yard.

It is important that you encourage risk taking in all subjects, but especially in math. Children who don't take risks limit their thinking to the known and/or someone else's answers. It is in the unknown that new potential lies. Encourage estimation. It is often in the act of approximating that the mind is doing its heaviest thinking. It's also important for children to look at mistakes positively, as a way to help them extend their learning.

Fourth grade is the grade when almost all of the children will be reading to learn rather than learning to read. Those fourth graders who can read well often gobble up books. Detective stories, mysteries, and biographies are often favorites. They love a period of silent reading each day with the book of their choice. This choice is important for two reasons: they will choose a book that has high interest; and they will choose one at their own reading level.

This is the stage when they often want to read every book in a series or every book by the same author. Because children can and do read on their own, parents often stop reading to them. It's still important to read together. Share your favorite prose or poetry.

Relationships and Emotions

Fourth graders center their relationships around "doing." With friends, their sense of camaraderie is high; it is what they *do* together that counts. An activity or goal is important. With family members, also, relationships often revolve around a shared interest or activity they do together, especially one that involves the learning or the perfecting of skills, such as golf, cooking, or woodworking. Even on a family excursion, nine-to-ten-year-olds like to have time alone with a parent to work on a skill.

In their emotional expression, as in the rest of their nature, fourth graders show much individuality. In general, they feel things deeply and are often worriers. Sometimes this apprehension appears as competitiveness and aggression; at other times, empathy and loyalty. For their best side to show, they must feel competent. Highly self-critical, and sometimes critical of others, the fourth grader is fiercely afraid of being criticized.

It's important for parents and teachers to realize how crucial it is for fourth graders to look good in the eyes of their peers. This doesn't have to take a competitive form. Looking good does not have to be at the expense of others. They can look good together: performing in a play, writing a book, working as a team. They can learn to laugh together. In fact, one of the ripening traits seen in nine-to-ten-year-olds is a developing and delightful sense of humor.

In fourth grade, many children are in a stage of marked mood swings. They have good days and bad days: days when they behave like adults; others, like children. Although they are usually loyal to their friends, there are days when even a best friend becomes an archenemy. For the most part, however, these flare-ups are short-lived. Some children go to extremes: they "love" something or they "hate it"; they're "good" at something or "terrible" at it.

This moodiness might take the form of complaining, especially about the body. Headaches and stomachaches are commonplace. Your child might complain about specific bodily distress, particularly if you ask him to do something he doesn't want to do. If you ask him to practice the piano, his hands might hurt. If you ask him to empty the trash, he might have a backache. These kinds of complaints are also heard at school, especially if things aren't going well or if he perceives schoolwork to be too difficult.

Ethics

Fourth graders are moving away from parents and teachers. "I'd rather do it myself and in my own way" sums up their attitude. This is often hard for parents, especially mothers, after the closeness of the third grade year. Fourth graders often seem more interested in friends than in family. Actually, they like to check things out with you, but they are very conscious of their peer group and want to live up to the standards of the group.

In most cases, these standards are good. Nine-to-ten-year-olds want to be responsible. They're working on establishing ethical guidelines and have a good sense of right and wrong. They try to do what's right, and they're critical of others who aren't doing right—according to *their* standards. They talk about honesty and the importance of being truthful.

Fourth graders get indignant when they sense injustice. "It's not fair!" is a refrain that rings out in the classroom and at home alike. It is very important to them that their parents and teachers be both fair and reasonable. They are aware of inequality in life and the unfairness of it. They feel deeply. Man's inhumanity to man is an issue with which they identify. They are now ready to struggle with some rather sophisticated social and ethical issues.

Discipline

Techniques of discipline that worked for younger children might no longer work with your fourth grader. Giving too many direct commands or insistence on total conformity can lead to outright rebellion or simply a deaf ear. "Choose your battles carefully" is an old and wise saying. Fourth graders want you to remember and respect their new maturity and their new independence. You might, however, be able to appeal to reason and logic. Humor (not sarcasm!) can also work wonders.

Some fourth graders love bartering. These children will readily negotiate. So you might trade a room cleanup for one of your child's jobs, such as cleaning off the table or emptying the garbage. The possibilities are endless. In fact, if you are good at the skill of negotiation yourself, you might offer to teach it to your child. Try for solutions where both you and your child are happy. Some fourth graders, however, are very good not only at negotiation but also at manipulation. It's not helpful to let them get away with it.

Your child also needs to take the consequences for the choices she makes. If she makes a good choice, the consequences will be good; if she makes a poor choice, the consequences will not be good. It will not be helpful to her in the long run for you to bail her out or to "rescue" her from these learning opportunities.

Fourth grade is a special year. Perhaps at no other stage is your child more ready to soak up skills, to become proficient. Mom and Dad, big sister or brother, even Grandma and Grandpa can be heroes in the life of the nine-to-ten-year-old if they are willing to share their skills. It doesn't really matter what the skill is. Perhaps it's hitting a baseball, making bread, or sharpening tools. Your reward will be your child's joy at having another talent to add to his repertoire. If you listen carefully, you might even hear the refrain of the fourth grader: "and then what—and then what?"

Questions and Answers About Fourth Grade

My child is a good student. He is involved in all sorts of extracurricular activities, and his teacher tells me he is doing just fine in class. What else should I be doing to make sure he excels?

First of all, give him time to play. More than anything, your child needs to have time for self-directed, open-ended activities of his own choosing. These are the activities that will foster the creativity, resilience, and flexibility of thought your child will need in the years ahead. Your child needs to build confidence in his own problem-solving abilities, to explore odd thoughts, and to risk making a few mistakes. No home tutoring program or extra credit homework, however creatively manufactured, can give him these skills. He must build them through experience.

Second, keep reading to your child. Many parents let the bedtime reading habit drop as soon as their children become independent readers. Don't let this happen. Throughout this book, you will hear the same refrain. If you do nothing else, read to your child. You will never regret the time.

Third, incorporate your child's learning into his and your natural interests. He might be interested in hockey or horses. You might be interested in gardening or computer graphics. Each of those interests includes opportunities for using math, reading, writing, and research skills. Share the interests, and your child will naturally build the skills.

My child has always been placed in reading groups, and although sometimes I haven't been very pleased about her placement, at least I've known where she stood in relation to the rest of the class. This year, the entire class—strong readers as well as weak readers—seems to be reading the same books. Should I complain?

First, talk to your child's teacher and try to get a sense of what kind of reading instruction is really going on in class. Aware of the many disadvantages of tracking children by ability, many teachers now use "flexible grouping," which means that they teach children in different groups for different purposes. Small groups (sometimes called literature groups) are usually temporary. One week, all of the children who are interested in a particular author might meet and read as a group. Another week, random groups of children get together to talk about plot in the separate books they're reading. Children who need particular skill work or need to focus on specific reading strategies meet for skill lessons. Flexible grouping keeps children from being labeled and allows children with different abilities and learning styles to learn from each other.

Homework has become a trial around our house. Any suggestions?

If you haven't done so already, establish a specific time and place—preferably when and where you're available—for homework to be done. Then, even if you are preparing dinner or reading quietly to younger children, you can supervise and provide help as needed. Your presence will also communicate your interest and faith in your child's schoolwork. Most fourth graders like company and are apt to stay more focused when you're nearby.

Beware, however; nine-to-ten-year-olds, above all, want to be independent. They want their homework to be just that, *theirs*. They want to be accountable, and they need to be. So refrain from helping until your child asks for it, and never do the work for him. Your best role is one of support.

If your child is having trouble with homework or any of his schoolwork, it's important to acknowledge this and take action *before* he's failing. Together with your child, solicit the help of his teacher. If all three of you plan together, you can set realistic goals and lay out a plan of action. Your child will feel supported, and he will be able to preserve his dignity and independence.

Whether homework consists of measuring the rooms in your house or studying spelling words, your fourth grader is beginning to establish habits that will last throughout his school career. Here are some additional tips to make sure those habits are good ones.

- Ask your child's teacher for a consistent homework routine. If your child knows that spelling words always come home on Tuesday, then both you and he can plan accordingly.
- Give your child a special homework folder. Papers stuffed into backpacks

often arrive home crumpled and torn. A pocket folder with a big HOME-WORK label on the front can help homework get to and from school relatively intact.

- Make sure your child has all the tools he needs in one place. He needs to know where he can find a ruler or scissors or a stapler if he requires one. Many a fourth grader has been found sorting through baseball cards when he was supposed to be looking for an eraser!

- Hang a calendar in your child's room and show him how to mark weekly or long-term assignments on it. Even marking "spelling test" on every Friday will prepare him for the more complicated homework scheduling to come. Help your child break homework assignments into smaller parts. For instance, it's better to memorize four spelling words a night than twenty words the night before the spelling test.

- Help your fourth grader come up with a list of homework rules. How many times can he pop up and down to get himself a snack? Is TV allowed before, after, or during homework time? If the homework assignment is open-ended (like interviewing parents about their jobs), how long is he allowed to spend on it?

- Finally, expect your child to take responsibility for getting his homework home and back to school, but do not underestimate the difficulty of this task. Make sure a part of each night's routine is getting homework into the backpack to be returned to school the next day.

If you put all of these routines in place, and your child is still unable to accomplish his homework, speak to his teacher. She may be able to make some adjustments.

My son insists on reading three or four books at a time. I'm sure he can't keep them all straight. How can I get him to read just one at a time?

Before you try to change your child's habits, look carefully at whether or not he is succeeding in his task. It could be that your child just learns differently than you do. Think about this example. You buy a new appliance at a department store. Before you leave the store, the salesperson tells you exactly how to install the appliance. What do you do when you get home?

If you go through the salesperson's words in your mind, most likely you are an auditory learner. You learn by listening. If, on the other hand, you go straight to the diagram in the instructions, you probably learn better visually. Finally, if you ignore the salesperson and the instructions and just plunge in with both hands, chances are you are a kinesthetic learner. You learn by doing.

Knowing your child's learning style (or, in the latest parlance, her type of intelligence or "how she is smart") can help you be more accepting of her "odd" ways of learning. Perhaps the three-book child makes sense of what he is reading by establishing connections among a number of different books.

For more information about different ways of learning, look for these books in your library:

- *Emotional Intelligence,* by Daniel Goleman (Bantam)
- *How Your Child Is Smart,* by Dawna Markova (Conary Press)
- *In Their Own Way: Discovering and Encouraging Your Child's Personal Learning Style,* by Thomas Armstrong (J. P. Tarcher)
- *Nurture by Nature,* by Paul D. Tieger and Barbara Barron-Tieger (Little, Brown)
- *Seven Pathways of Learning: Teaching Students and Parents about Multiple Intelligences,* by David Lazear (Zephyr Press)
- *Teaching Students to Read Through Their Individual Learning Styles,* by Marie Carbo, Rita Dunn, and Kenneth Dunn (Reston)
- *Unicorns are Real,* by Barbara Meister Vitale (Warner)

How to Use This Book

Using the Parent Observation Pages and the For Kids Only Booklet

Assessment is a natural process for parents. Every time you asked your young child a question—"Can you say Dada?" "Where is your nose?" "What color is this?"—you were collecting information and using that information to determine what to teach your child next. If you had questions about your child's development, you asked your pediatrician or consulted a checklist of developmental stages of learning. By observing your child and asking the right questions, you were able to support your child's learning.

Now that your child is school-aged, however, you might find it harder to maintain the role of supportive coach. It's a greater challenge to get a clear understanding of what is expected of your child. Without specific knowledge of the curriculum, you might not know what questions to ask. The purpose of this book, and of the accompanying assessment, is to help you to observe your child with awareness again.

The word *assessment* comes from roots that mean "to sit beside." The informal assessment is a way for you to sit beside your child and collect the information you need. After you have observed your child, you will be guided to activities that will encourage you and your child to continue to learn together.

Remember, the assessment is not a standardized test. It will not tell you how your child compares to other children in the nation. It will not even tell you how your child compares with your neighbor's child. But it will give you a starting point for determining how to increase your child's confidence and success in learning. Instructions for participating in the assessment are as follows:

1. **Take the "For Kids Only" booklet out of the envelope in the back of the book and read through it one time.** This will familiarize you with the visuals that you will be presenting your child.

2. **Photocopy and read the Parent Observation Pages** (page 34). Reading these pages ahead of time will help you to see how the child's booklet and your instructions are coordinated. It will also allow you to determine how long it might take your child to complete it. For the fourth grade assessment we recommend doing an activity here or there over at least a week's time. As you will see, the reading section requires your immediate participation. You will probably be able to complete this section in one thirty-minute sitting. The writing and the math assessments can be done independently by your child and will require, considering a fourth grader's busy schedule and the thoroughness of the assessment, several relaxed sessions. Remember, most fourth graders like to take their time and complete an activity carefully.

   Keep in mind also that this book covers the skills your child will be introduced to over a full year of learning. If you give your child the assessment at the beginning of the school year, the results will obviously be different than if you give the assessment at the end of the year. Teachers introduce the material at different times. So don't be anxious if your child tells you that he's never heard of an idiom or a right angle. Be pleased that you can introduce these terms in a fun and lively way at home.

3. **Provide a place to give the assessment that is relatively free of distractions.** Show your child how the assessment works. Tell your child that you want to learn more about him and that these activities will teach *you*. Let him know that after he completes the assessment, the book will direct you both to fun activities. Make sure you approach the activity in a lighthearted manner.

4. **Above all, keep the assessment fun and relaxed for your child.** If your child is afraid to try an activity, don't push him. After all, that is valuable information for you, too. Whenever your child has difficulty with a reading passage or a math problem, *stop* and skip ahead to the question directed (or the one that immediately follows). There is never a reason to work beyond your child's comfort level.

5. **Give positive reinforcement as often as possible.** You might just say, "I didn't know you could do that!" If your child seems upset or confused

by an exercise, let him off the hook. You might say, "That question is real confusing, isn't it?" Make sure your child ends the assessment feeling successful. One way of doing this is to return to a question your child could answer with obvious ease. Say, "I forgot to write your answer down. Can you show me how you did this problem again?"

Using the Assessment Guide

The assessment guide (page 52) will allow you to find out what your child knows and what he is ready to learn next. If you find that a question on the assessment did not give you enough information or if you are confused about your child's response, you might want to talk to your child's teacher. See Working with Your Child's Teacher (page 196) for more information.

Using the Suggested Activities

In each skill area, activities are suggested under two headings: "Have Five Minutes?" and "Have More Time?" Some of the activities in the five-minute section are quick games that you and your child can play while waiting for dinner, riding in the car, or walking to the bus stop. Others are activities that you can explain in less than five minutes and then let your child complete on his own. Activities in the "Have More Time?" category require more planning or a longer time commitment on your part.

Do not feel that you should do every activity listed under a skill heading. A number of different activities are provided so you can pick and choose the ones that appeal to you and your child. And don't feel guilty if you haven't tried something new for a while. If you do only a couple of these activities occasionally, you will be giving your fourth grader a genuine boost toward success. You'll be amazed at how a question here or a three-minute activity there can demonstrate to your child how much you value his ideas and his education. Feel free to adapt these activities to your needs.

Even if you are not directed to a specific section, you might want to try some of the activities in that section. Reviewing has wonderful benefits. When your child revisits a skill, he usually gains a deeper understanding that he can apply to new learning. In every area there are sure to be games that your child will enjoy playing.

Should you pursue activities that seem more difficult? Probably not. Pushing your child too fast might backfire. Instead of looking forward to the games you initiate, your child might associate them with confusion, boredom, or failure. It's good to remember that success is the greatest motivator of all.

Some of the activities are competitive. Some fourth grade children do not care for competitive games. If your child is one, make the activity noncompetitive. Rather than playing against each other, make yourselves a team and try to beat the clock or another imaginary player—who always makes the most ridiculous decisions!

Reassess

Repeat the assessment when appropriate.

After some time has gone by—perhaps two or three months—and you and your child have participated in many of the activities, you might want to give the assessment or a portion of it again. By reassessing, you can determine if your child has grown in his understanding of concepts. It's possible that the Assessment Guide (page 52) will direct you to new areas of learning to focus on next.

If you choose not to give the entire assessment a second time, make sure you ask some questions that you know your child will answer competently. *Always end the assessment on a positive note.*

Remember, the assessment is meant to be an informal tool for gathering information. You might want to adapt the questions or ask new questions to see if your fourth grader has truly mastered a skill.

Many teachers now assess children in the classroom by doing what one educator termed kid watching. Kid watching is what parents have always done best. Have a ball watching your child grasp new knowledge.

Parent Observation Pages

Photocopy the Parent Observation Pages. Taking the time to photocopy the pages will allow you to match your child's responses to the answer guide more easily. It will also allow you to repeat the assessment on your child or to give the assessment to a sibling.

Ask your child the questions that appear in italics throughout the assessment; however, do not feel that you must rigidly adhere to the wording here. These questions are meant as a guide, not a script. You might find other ways of questioning that are more suited to your own and your child's needs. For more information, see the preceding chapter, "How to Use this Book."

Reading Assessment

**How the Fly Saved
the Great River**

Long ago, when everything was new, all the water in the world was in one Great River. All the animals loved this river. Beavers built their houses in its clear pools. Fish glided in and out of its rushing waters. Raccoons and otters dug for food in its muddy banks.

One day, a thirsty moose came to drink at the Great River. The moose was so big, and he drank so much water, that the river began to disappear before the other animals' very eyes!

"This is terrible!" cried the animals. "What will happen to our homes and families? Without water, we will all surely die!"

The animals agreed that they had to get rid of the moose, but who would do the job? Even the grizzly bear was no match for the giant moose.

Finally, a tiny fly buzzed, "I will do it. I will drive the giant moose away."▲

The rest of the animals looked at the tiny fly and jeered. "YOU? How can someone your size drive away a giant moose?"

As quick as a wink, the fly flew over and lit upon the moose's nose. Then he bit with all his might. The moose shook his head, snorted, and stamped his hoof. But the fly just flitted to the moose's ear and gave it an even sharper bite. The more the moose stamped and snorted, the harder the fly bit. Finally, the poor moose ran away from the river just to get away from the pesky fly. And the moose was never seen at the Great River again.

2

3

Use assessment booklet pages 2–3 for questions 1–3.

1. **Use pages 2 and 3 of the booklet.** Say, *Read this story aloud to here* (point to the black triangle). If your child stops at a word, give him or her a moment to figure it out, then supply the word if necessary.
   What does your child do to figure out a word he or she doesn't know?
   Check all that apply.
   ___ Sounds it out.
   ___ Divides the word into syllables.
   ___ Guesses based on context.
   ___ Skips the word and then goes back.
   ___ Knew all the words.

2. When your child reaches the triangle, ask, *What do you think will happen next?*
   Check one.
   ___ Makes a prediction.
   ___ Does not make a prediction.
   Ask, *What makes you think that this is going to happen?*
   ___ Gives reasoning behind prediction.
   ___ Does not give reasoning or clues.

3. *Continue reading so that we can see what happens.*
   Can your child answer these questions? (He or she may refer back to the story if necessary.) Check all **correct** answers.

   ___ A. What happened in this story? (A giant moose threatened to drink up all the water in the Great River. A fly drove the moose away by pestering him.)

   ___ B. What does the word *jeered* mean? (laughed at)

   ___ C. Obijibway (O-be-ja-way) Indians told this legend long ago. Why do you think they told this legend? (Check if your child attempts to answer the question.)

   ___ D. Can you think of any other ways the animals could have solved their problem? (Check if your child attempts to answer the question.)

   ___ E. Can you find a synonym (a word that has almost the same meaning) for the word *big* in this story? (giant, huge)

   ___ F. Look at the word *disappear*. What root (base) word do you see within that word? (appear) Can you tell me any other words that have *appear* as their root? (appearing, disappearance, reappear, etc.)

   ___ G. If this story had a moral like one of Aesop's Fables, what do you think it would be? (Check if your child attempts to come up with a moral. Possibilities might include *Good thinking matters more than great size* or *You don't need a big voice to have a good idea.*)

> **I**f your child stopped at fewer than 5 words in the previous story, allow him or her to read the next story silently. If your child stopped at 5–8 words, ask him or her to read the next story aloud. If your child stopped at more than 8 words, STOP here and proceed to question 7.

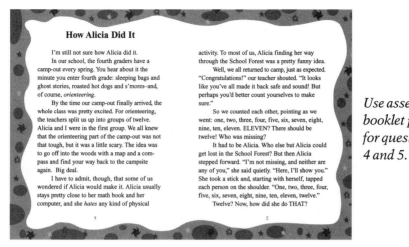

How Alicia Did It

I'm still not sure how Alicia did it.

In our school, the fourth graders have a camp-out every spring. You hear about it the minute you enter fourth grade: sleeping bags and ghost stories, roasted hot dogs and s'mores–and, of course, *orienteering*.

By the time our camp-out finally arrived, the whole class was pretty excited. For orienteering, the teachers split us up into groups of twelve. Alicia and I were in the first group. We all knew that the orienteering part of the camp-out was not that tough, but it was a little scary. The idea was to go off into the woods with a map and a compass and find your way back to the campsite again. Big deal.

I have to admit, though, that some of us wondered if Alicia would make it. Alicia usually stays pretty close to her math book and her computer, and she *hates* any kind of physical activity. To most of us, Alicia finding her way through the School Forest was a pretty funny idea.

Well, we all returned to camp, just as expected. "Congratulations!" our teacher shouted. "It looks like you've all made it back safe and sound! But perhaps you'd better count yourselves to make sure."

So we counted each other, pointing as we went: one, two, three, four, five, six, seven, eight, nine, ten, eleven. ELEVEN? There should be twelve! Who was missing?

It had to be Alicia. Who else but Alicia could get lost in the School Forest? But then Alicia stepped forward. "I'm not missing, and neither are any of you," she said quietly. "Here, I'll show you." She took a stick and, starting with herself, tapped each person on the shoulder. "One, two, three, four, five, six, seven, eight, nine, ten, eleven, twelve."

Twelve? Now, how did she do THAT?

Use assessment booklet pages 4–5 for questions 4 and 5.

4. **Use with pages 4 and 5 of the booklet.** *Now read this story.* If your child stops at a word (if reading aloud) or asks for help with a word (if reading silently), give him or her a moment to figure it out, then supply the word if necessary.

   When your child reaches the end of the story ask, *What do you think Alicia did?*

   Check one.

   ___ Tries to draw a conclusion.

   ___ Does not try to draw a conclusion.

5. Can your child answer these questions? (He or she may refer back to the story if necessary.) Check all **correct** answers.

   ___ A. Can you tell me, in just a few sentences, what happened in this story? (The kids went on a campout and thought someone got lost. Then it turned out that they had counted incorrectly.)

   ___ B. What is orienteering? (An activity in which people find their way from one place to another using only a map and a compass.)

   ___ C. How many syllables does the word *orienteering* have? (5) How would you split that word into syllables? (or-i-en-teer-ing)

   ___ D. Why did the kids think that Alicia's finding her way through the forest was a pretty funny idea? (Check if your child attempts to answer the question.)

   ___ E. Do you think the other kids treated Alicia fairly? Why or why not? (Check if your child attempts to answer the question.)

   ___ F. What did Alicia do that the other children did not do? (She counted herself.)

___ G. Do you think Alicia and the fly from the previous story are alike in any way? How? (One possible response: they both use their brains to figure out problems. Check if your child attempts to answer the question.)

> If your child stopped at fewer than 5 words in the previous story, allow him or her to read the next section silently. If your child stopped at 5–8 words, ask him or her to read the letter aloud. If your child stopped at more than 8 words, STOP here and proceed to question 7.

Use assessment booklet pages 6–7 for question 6.

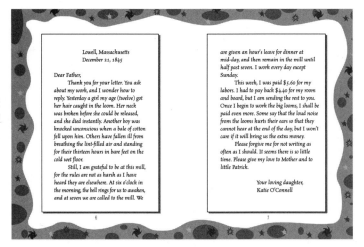

Lowell, Massachusetts
December 21, 1845

Dear Father,
Thank you for your letter. You ask about my work, and I wonder how to reply. Yesterday a girl my age (twelve) got her hair caught in the loom. Her neck was broken before she could be released, and she died instantly. Another boy was knocked unconscious when a bale of cotton fell upon him. Others have fallen ill from breathing the lint-filled air and standing for their thirteen hours in bare feet on the cold wet floor.
Still, I am grateful to be at this mill, for the rules are not as harsh as I have heard they are elsewhere. At six o'clock in the morning, the bell rings for us to awaken, and at seven we are called to the mill. We

are given an hour's leave for dinner at mid-day, and then remain in the mill until half past seven. I work every day except Sunday.
This week, I was paid $5.60 for my labors. I had to pay back $4.40 for my room and board, but I am sending the rest to you. Once I begin to work the big looms, I shall be paid even more. Some say that the loud noise from the looms hurts their ears so that they cannot hear at the end of the day, but I won't care if it will bring us the extra money.
Please forgive me for not writing as often as I should. It seems there is so little time. Please give my love to Mother and to little Patrick.

Your loving daughter,
Katie O'Connell

6   7

6. **Use pages 6 and 7 of the booklet.** If your child stops at a word (if reading aloud) or asks for help with a word (if reading silently), give him or her a moment to figure it out, then supply the word if necessary.

Can your child answer these questions? (He or she may refer back to the letter if necessary.) Check all **correct** answers.

___ A. What form is this passage written in (story, poem, article, letter, biography, etc.)? (letter) When was it written? (1845)

___ B. How do you think Katie feels about working at the mill? (Check if your child's answer shows an awareness of the information in the text: She doesn't like it, but she thinks she should do it; she thinks it's dangerous; she likes the money; and so on.)

___ C. What are some details that tell you that mill work is dangerous? (A girl's hair got caught in the loom. A bale of cotton fell on a boy. The mill is noisy and wet and cold.)

___ D. What words would you use to describe the girl? (Obedient, overworked, lonely, poor, etc. Check if your child attempts to answer the question.)

___ E. Do you think a girl like Katie really could have written this letter? Why or why not? (Check if your child attempts to answer the question.)

___ F. What do you think could have been done to help Katie? (Check if your child attempts to answer the question.)

___ G. How is your life the same as Katie's? How is it different? (Check if your child attempts to answer the question.)

___ H. If you wanted to find more information about millworkers in the 1800s, where would you look? (If your child answers "The library," ask, "Where would you look in the library?" Correct responses might include: the card catalog, the computer (catalog, encyclopedia, or Internet), the nonfiction shelves, the encyclopedia, specific books, the reference librarian, or other experts.)

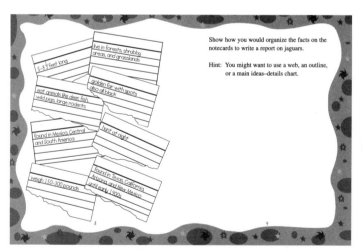

Use assessment booklet pages 8–9 for question 7.

7. *Read the information on the notecards. If you had to organize the information on these cards to write a report, how would you do it? If you want, use another sheet of paper to show how you would organize the information. Remember, you do* not *have to use all the information on all of the notecards!*

Check all that apply.
___ Could organize the information.
___ Had difficulty categorizing the information.
___ Divided information into main ideas and details.
___ Cannot organize this kind of material at this time.

8. What are your child's reading habits? Please check all that apply.
   ___ Listens to me or another adult read on a regular basis.
   ___ Reads to himself or herself daily.
   ___ Is interested in a wide range of reading materials. (nonfiction, fiction, magazines)
   ___ Searches books or magazines for answers to questions.
   ___ Likes to predict what will happen in a story.
   ___ Talks about a story as he or she reads it or when the story is completed.

The Your Turn! survey on page 10 of the booklet will also help you to assess your child's reading skills, comfort level, and needs. You will want to have it handy when using the Assessment Guide on page 52.

Writing Assessment

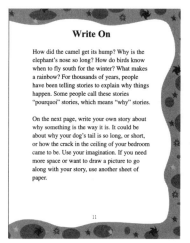

Write On

How did the camel get its hump? Why is the elephant's nose so long? How do birds know when to fly south for the winter? What makes a rainbow? For thousands of years, people have been telling stories to explain why things happen. Some people call these stories "pourquoi" stories, which means "why" stories.

On the next page, write your own story about why something is the way it is. It could be about why your dog's tail is so long, or short, or how the crack in the ceiling of your bedroom came to be. Use your imagination. If you need more space or want to draw a picture to go along with your story, use another sheet of paper.

11

Use assessment booklet page 11 for question 1.

Have your child read and follow the directions on pages 10 and 11 of the "For Kids Only" booklet.

1. Does your child's story show the following? (Check all that apply.)
   ___ A. Approached this writing task with confidence.
   ___ B. Considered the purpose of the story.
   ___ C. Used imagination in creating the story.
   ___ D. Expressed ideas clearly and in logical sequence.
   ___ E. Wrote complete sentences.
   ___ F. Avoided run-on sentences (long sentences that could be divided into a number of shorter sentences; run-on sentences usually contain too many *and*s or *but*s).
   ___ G. Used paragraph form.
   ___ H. Paragraphs began with a topic sentence and were followed by supporting details.
   ___ I. Used capitalization and punctuation properly.
   ___ J. Used conventional spellings 75–90 percent of the time.
   ___ K. Took risks by using words that might or might not be spelled correctly.
   ___ L. Used cursive writing.

Your Turn Again!

Do you like to write?
Yes, because_____.
No, because_____.

There are lots of different types of writing. Give each of the types of writing below a number. Here are what the numbers mean:

1 – I love to write these.   3 – I hate to write these.
2 – Sometimes I like to write these.   4 – I never tried writing these.

____ stories   ____ reports   ____ secret stuff in my diary
____ poems   ____ letters

Have you ever done research before? ____ yes ____ no

If you found a strange-looking rock in front of your house, how would you go about trying to identify it?
_____
_____

Are you a good speller?
____ very good ____ okay ____ not very good ____ terrible

Do you usually write in cursive writing?
____ yes
____ no, I never learned it well enough.
____ no, I don't like to, because_____.

Have you ever given an oral presentation before?
____ yes ____ no

13

The Your Turn Again! survey on page 13 of the booklet will also help you to assess your child's writing skills, comfort level, and needs. You will want to have it handy when using the Assessment Guide on page 52.

Math Assessment

Before beginning the math assessment, have paper and pencil available for your child to use. You may also wish to have a calculator to check your child's computation. If your child has difficulty reading any of the math problems in the "For Kids Only" booklet, go ahead and read the passages aloud.

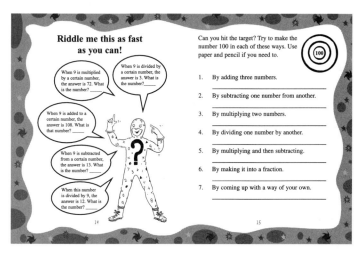

Use assessment booklet pages 14–15 for questions 1 and 2.

1. **Use page 14 of the booklet.** *Can you solve the Riddler's problems?* Check **correct** answers.
   ___ When 9 is subtracted from a certain number, the answer is 13. What is the number? (22)
   ___ When 9 is multiplied by a certain number, the answer is 72. What is the number? (8)
   ___ When 9 is added to a certain number, the answer is 108. What is the number? (99)
   ___ When 9 is divided by a certain number, the answer is 3. What is the number? (3)
   ___ When 9 is divided into a certain number, the answer is 12. What is the number? (108)
   How did your child work out the problems?
   ___ In his or her head.
   ___ With paper and pencil.
   ___ Both.

2. **Use page 15 of the booklet.** *Can you make 100 in each of these ways?*
Check all that apply.
___ A. Read and understood each target challenge.
___ B. Came up with a plan for reaching the target each time.
___ C. Expressed confidence (or seemed confident) while attempting to
solve the problems.
___ D. Persisted until each solution was found.
___ E. Checked the accuracy of the solutions without prompting.
___ F. Was able to compute accurately.

*Use assessment
booklet pages
16–17 for
question 3.*

3. **Use pages 16–17 of the booklet.** *Can you solve the Riddler's problem?*
Talk to your child to find out how he or she solved the problem. Check all
that apply.
___ A. Read and understood the problem.
___ B. Came up with a plan for solving the problem.
___ C. Expressed confidence (or seemed confident) while attempting to
solve the problem.
___ D. Used one or more of the following strategies:
(Please check one or more)
___ used objects
___ drew a picture
___ made a chart
___ made an organized list
___ looked for a pattern
___ worked backwards

___ thought of a simpler problem
___ guessed and checked
___ used logical reasoning
___ E. Persisted until a solution was found.
___ F. Found 3 different combinations to solve the problem.
___ G. Checked the accuracy of the solutions without prompting.
___ H. Understood the money values in the problem.
___ I. Was able to add money values successfully.

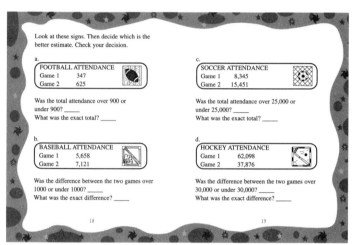

Use assessment booklet pages 18–19 for question 4.

4. **Use pages 18–19 of the booklet.** *Which is the better estimate?* Check all **correct** responses.

a. ___ Estimate (over 900)
   ___ Exact total (972)
b. ___ Estimate (over 1,000)
   ___ Exact difference (1,463)
c. ___ Estimate (under 25,000)
   ___ Exact total (23,796)
d. ___ Estimate (under 30,000)
   ___ Exact difference (24,222)

*Use assessment
booklet pages
20–21 for
questions 5 and 6.*

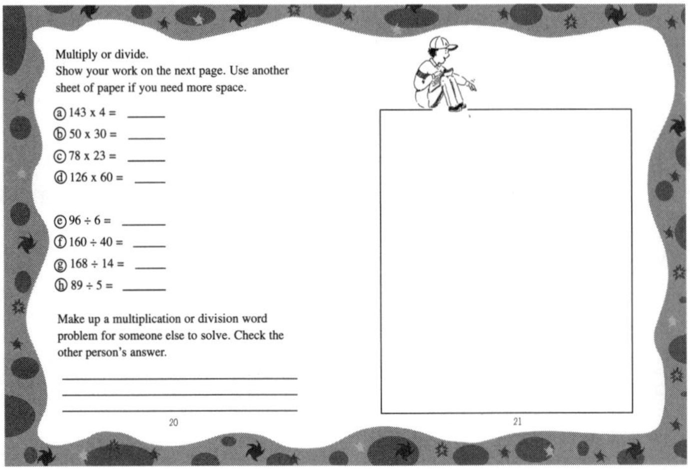

Multiply or divide.
Show your work on the next page. Use another
sheet of paper if you need more space.

(a) 143 x 4 = _____
(b) 50 x 30 = _____
(c) 78 x 23 = _____
(d) 126 x 60 = _____

(e) 96 ÷ 6 = _____
(f) 160 ÷ 40 = _____
(g) 168 ÷ 14 = _____
(h) 89 ÷ 5 = _____

Make up a multiplication or division word
problem for someone else to solve. Check the
other person's answer.

_____
_____
_____

20   21

5. **Use pages 20–21 of the booklet.** *Can you solve these problems?*
   Circle all **correct** answers.
   a. 572
   b. 1,500
   c. 1,794
   d. 7,560
   e. 16
   f. 4
   g. 12
   h. 17 R 4 *or* 17 4/5

   Check all that apply.
   ___ Solved multiplication problems correctly.
   ___ Attempted to solve multiplication problems but made errors.
   ___ Cannot do multiplication at this time.
   ___ Solved division problems correctly.
   ___ Attempted to solve division problems but made errors.
   ___ Cannot do division at this time.

6. *Write a multiplication or division word problem for me to solve.* After your
   child has written a problem, try to solve it. Then check all that apply:
   ___ A. Did not want to attempt to write a problem.
   ___ B. Began to write a problem but did not know how to incorporate
   multiplication or division as the task.
   ___ C. Wrote a problem that calls for a function other than multiplication
   or division.

___ D. Wrote a story, but did not phrase it as a problem.

___ E. Wrote a problem that does not contain enough information.

___ F. Wrote a word problem (ending in a question) that can be solved by multiplying or dividing.

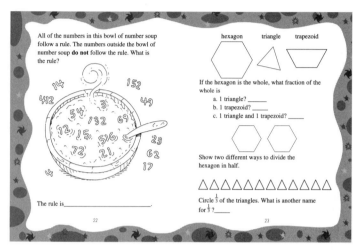

Use assessment booklet pages 22–23 for questions 7 and 8.

7. **Use page 22 of the booklet.** *Can you solve this problem?*

___ Gave correct rule. (The numbers are all divisible by 3.)

___ Attempted problem, but could not come up with rule at this time.

___ Did not attempt to solve problem.

8. **Use page 23 of the booklet.** *Can you solve these problems?* Circle all **correct** answers.

a. 1/6

b. 1/2

c. 4/6 *or* 2/3

Show me two ways to divide the hexagon in half. Check that portions are equal in both drawings.

___ Showed one way.

___ Showed more than one way.

___ Could not do this problem at this time.

Can you circle 1/3 of the triangles? (4 triangles) *What is another name for 1/3?* (4/12, 2/6, and so on)

___ Answered both questions correctly.

___ Could not answer one or both of these questions at this time.

*Use assessment
booklet pages
24–25 for
questions
9 and 10.*

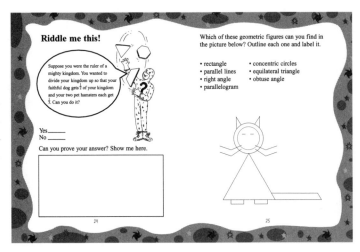

9. **Use page 24 of the booklet.** *Can you solve the Riddler's problem?*
   Talk to your child to find out how he or she solved the problem. Check all
   that apply.
   ___ A. Read and understood the problem.
   ___ B. Came up with a plan for solving the problem.
   ___ C. Expressed confidence (or seemed confident) while attempting to
   solve the problem.
   ___ D. Used one or more of the following strategies:
   (Please check one or more)
   ___ used objects
   ___ drew a picture
   ___ made a chart
   ___ looked for a pattern
   ___ guessed and checked
   ___ used logical reasoning
   ___ E. Persisted until a solution was found. (No, the kingdom cannot be
   divided in this way.)
   ___ F. Demonstrated reasonableness of solution.

10. **Use page 25 of the booklet.** *Can you find and label these geometric
   figures?* Check all that apply.

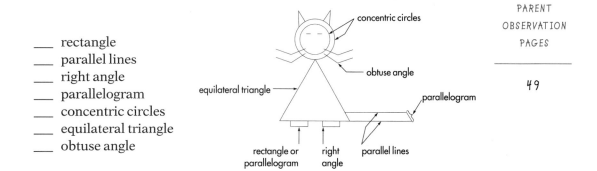

____ rectangle
____ parallel lines
____ right angle
____ parallelogram
____ concentric circles
____ equilateral triangle
____ obtuse angle

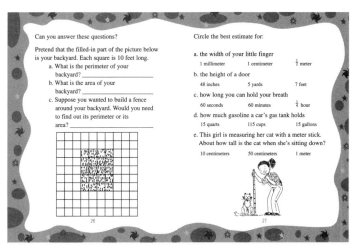

*Use assessment
booklet pages
26–27 for
questions
11 and 12.*

11. **Use page 26 of the booklet.** *Can you answer the questions?* Check all that apply.
    ____ Determined the perimeter of the yard. (180 feet)
    ____ Determined the area of the yard. (200 square feet)
    ____ Knew how to measure perimeter or area but did not find correct measures.
    ____ Answered correctly that the fence needs a measure of perimeter.
    ____ Has not been introduced to perimeter or area at this time.

12. **Use page 27 of the booklet.** *Can you choose the correct estimate for each of these things?* Circle all **correct** answers.
    a.   1 centimeter
    b.   7 feet
    c.   60 seconds
    d.   5 gallons
    e.   50 centimeters

*Use assessment
booklet pages
28–29 for
question 13.*

> Look at the butterflies on the opposite page.
> Then answer the questions.
>
> a.   About how many butterflies do you think are
>   on the page? _____
> b.   Now count. How many are there? _____
> c.   How many butterflies are shaded? _____
> d.   What fraction of the butterflies are
>   shaded? _____
> e.   What is the decimal name for that
>   fraction? _____
> f.   What percentage of the butterflies are
>   shaded? _____
> g.   What percentage of the butterflies are *not*
>   shaded? _____
>
>   28   29

13. **Use pages 28–29 of the booklet.** *Can you answer these questions?* Check all that apply.

    ___ A. Can estimate within 20 how many butterflies are on the page. (80–120) (Using strategies for estimating—such as counting the number of butterflies in the top row and multiplying that number by the number of butterflies in the first column—are acceptable.)

    ___ B. Can make an accurate count. (100)

    ___ C. Can determine how many butterflies are shaded. (25)

    ___ D. Can determine what fraction of the butterflies are shaded. (25/100 or 1/4)

    ___ E. Can write a decimal for 25/100. (.25)

    ___ F. Can determine what percentage of the butterflies are shaded. (25%)

    ___ G. Can determine what percentage of the butterflies are *not* shaded. (75%)

    ___ H. Has not been introduced to decimals at this time.

    ___ I. Has not been introduced to percentages at this time.

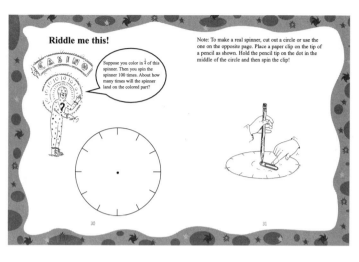

*Use assessment
booklet pages
30–31 for
question 14.*

14. **Use page 30–31 of the booklet.** *Can you answer the Riddler's questions?*
Talk to your child to find out how he or she solved the problem. Check all
that apply.

___ A. Read and understood the problem.

___ B. Came up with a plan for solving the problem.

___ C. Expressed confidence (or seemed confident) while attempting to
solve the problem.

___ D. Used one or more of the following strategies:
(Please check one or more)

   ___ used objects

   ___ drew a picture

   ___ made a chart

   ___ made an organized list

   ___ looked for a pattern

   ___ worked backwards

   ___ thought of a simpler problem

   ___ guessed and checked

   ___ used logical reasoning

___ E. Persisted until the problem was solved.

___ F. Found the correct solution to the problem. (about 25)

___ G. Performed a probability experiment to check the accuracy of the
solution without prompting.

___ H. Recognized that 1/4 is equal to 25 out of 100 or 25%.

Assessment Guide

This assessment guide will tell you what the data you've collected on the Parent Observation form means. It will also direct you to the activity sections in the book that are most appropriate for *your* fourth grader.

Reading Assessment

Question 1

This question will help you determine which strategies your child uses to decode words. If your child is relying on strategies that don't seem to be working, see Reading Comprehension, page 59; Word Study, page 89; and Spelling, page 111. If your child struggled through most of this passage, you may also want to see Struggling Readers, page 98. If your child could read this passage with ease, it's likely that he or she uses a number of successful approaches to reading.

Question 2

This question helps you determine whether your child is comfortable making predictions as he or she reads. If your child was reluctant about making a prediction or could not back the prediction up with logical reasoning or clues from the story, see Reading Comprehension, page 59.

Question 3

These questions help you to determine whether or not your child understands what he or she reads.

Question A asks your child to recall the events of the story in correct sequence.

Question B asks a vocabulary question. If your child did not know this word prior to reading this passage, Question B will help you determine whether or not your child uses context clues to figure out the meaning of new words.

Question C asks about the author's purpose in telling the story.

Question D encourages your child to use critical thinking skills to synthesize and extend the meaning of the text.

Question E determines your child's ability to identify synonyms within the text.

Question F asks your child to apply and extend his or her decoding skills.

Question G asks your child to draw conclusions from what he or she has read.

If your child could read the words but had difficulty answering Questions A, C, D, and G, see Reading Comprehension, page 59. If your child had difficulty with Questions B and E, see Vocabulary, page 84. If your child had trouble with Question F, see Word Study, page 89. If your child particularly enjoyed answering Questions D and G, see Reading and Writing Enrichment on pages 116–19 for activities that support and extend your child's reading and writing.

Question 4

Good readers are constantly thinking about and drawing conclusions based on what they have read. If your child was reluctant to talk about what he or she thought Alicia did in the story or if you think he or she could use more practice in this skill, see Reading Comprehension, page 59.

Question 5

Again, these questions will help you to determine how well your fourth grader understands what he or she reads.

Question A asks that your child summarize the story.

Question B asks another vocabulary question. If your child has not heard the word *orienteering,* could he or she determine the meaning from the context of the story?

Question C helps you determine your child's ability to break large words into smaller syllables, a very useful decoding skill.

Question D encourages your child to draw a conclusion.

Question E encourages your child to make a judgment.

Question F asks your child to draw a conclusion based on important details in the text.

Question G invites your child to compare and contrast.

If your child had difficulty with Questions A, D, E, F, or G, see Reading Comprehension, page 59. If your child had difficulty with Question B or C, see Vocabulary, page 84, and Word Study, page 89. If your child enjoyed answering Question G, you might want to try some of the activities in Reading and Writing Enrichment, page 116.

Question 6

These questions assess your child's comprehension and knowledge of historical action in a letter format.

Questions A asks your child to identify the form of writing and information from one of its parts.

Question B asks your child to make inferences based on information in the text.

Question C asks your child to identify details that lead to a conclusion.

Question D asks your child to synthesize information and make judgments.

Question E asks your child to distinguish between realism and fantasy.

Question F asks your child to extend his or her critical thinking beyond the scope of the text.

Question G asks your child to compare and contrast.

Question H helps you determine your child's research skills.

If your child had difficulty with Questions A through G, see Reading Comprehension, page 59. If your child had difficulty answering Question H, see Study Skills, page 94.

Question 7

The ability to collect and organize information is the cornerstone of report writing and oral presentations. Question 7 asks your child to organize information in any way that makes sense to him or her. Most fourth graders are just beginning to build research skills. If you feel your child could use more support in research and study skills, see Study Skills, page 91.

Question 8

Question 8 surveys your child's reading habits. These are the habits exhibited by growing, enthusiastic readers. If you did not check at least four of these habits, you might want to see Reading Comprehension, page 59. If you checked only one or two of these habits, you might also want to see Struggling Readers, page 98.

Writing Assessment

Knowing where your child is in the process of learning to write will help you respond to written work and support his or her growth as a writer. If you have any concerns about Questions A–D or the survey your child completed, see Prewriting and Writing, pages 106 and 108. If you have any concerns about Questions E–L, see Revising and Editing, pages 107 and 108. Remember, writing and reading skills naturally reinforce one another. Help your child to become a better writer and you will help him or her to become a better reader as well.

Math Assessment

Question 1

By fourth grade, your child should be able to solve simple computation problems involving addition, subtraction, multiplication, and division quickly and accurately. If you feel your child could use more practice in these basic skills, see Number Sense, page 135; Multiplication, page 151; and Division, page 157.

Question 2

To be truly successful in math, children must develop proficiency in problem solving. They must develop strategies to help them comprehend problems, seek solutions, and identify reasonable answers. They need to learn that problem solving requires inquiry and persistence but can be genuinely fun, too.

If you did not check A–F, see Problem Solving, page 120, for ways to help your child grow as a problem solver.

If you did not check D–F, see Number Sense, page 135, in addition to Problem Solving.

If your child had difficulty with a specific computation skill (1–7 in the "For Kids Only" booklet), see the following sections:

Problems 1–2: see Number Sense, page 135;

Problems 3 and 5: see Multiplication, page 151

Problem 4: see Division, page 157;

Problem 6: see Fractions, page 162.

Question 3

This question gives you another chance to assess your child's problem-solving skills and will help you to determine which computation processes your fourth grader is most comfortable using. Watch to see if your child is developing a repertoire of strategies.

If you did not check A–E, see Problem Solving, page 120, for ways to help your child grow as a problem solver.

If you did not check F–I, see Number Sense, page 135, in addition to Problem Solving.

If you did not check H–I, see Decimals, page 166, in addition to Problem Solving and Number Sense.

Question 4

By fourth grade your child should demonstrate an ability to work with numbers through the hundred thousands—estimating, adding, and subtracting. If your child could not estimate the sum or the difference (within 20) on any of these questions, see Number Sense, page 135.

Question 5

To multiply and divide numbers effectively, your child needs a strong understanding of place value and a quick and accurate recall of multiplication and division facts. This question assesses your child's understanding of place value and flexibility in multiplying and dividing numbers. If you did *not* circle any of answers a–d, see Multiplication, page 151. If you did not circle any of answers e–h, see Division, page 157.

Question 6

An understanding of the relationships among numbers and recognition of patterns is fundamental to mathematics, including all computation. If your child had difficulty discovering this rule, or if you would like to strengthen his or her understanding of numbers and their relationships, see Number Sense, page 135.

Question 7

It's important that fourth graders go beyond learning multiplication and division methods as "tricks" to be memorized. They need to be able to apply their knowledge to problem solving. Writing a multiplication or division word problem asks your child to demonstrate his or her understanding of these concepts of multiplication. If you checked A–C, see Multiplication, page 151, or Division, page 157, for activity suggestions. If you checked D or E, it is likely that your child could use more practice in problem solving. See page 120. If you checked F, you might want to explore some of the activities in Math Enrichment, page 186.

Question 8

Fourth graders need a strong understanding of basic fraction concepts and equivalencies before they can move on to the rigorous work of fraction computation in fifth grade. If your child had difficulty with any of these problems, or to reinforce fraction concepts, see Fractions, page 162.

Question 9

This question gives you another chance to assess your child's problem-solving skills and will help you to determine your child's understanding of how fractions work. Watch to see if your child is developing a repertoire of strategies in solving this problem.

If you did not check A–F, see Problem Solving, page 120.

If you did not check E or F, you will want to give your child more hands-on experience with basic fraction concepts. See Fractions, page 162.

If you checked E and F, or if your child solved the problem using quick logical reasoning, you might also want to see the activities in the Math Enrichment section, page 186.

Question 10

This year, your child will move beyond the simple recognition of shapes and learn a wide range of geometric concepts and terms. To support this work, see Geometry, page 169.

Question 11

Measuring area and perimeter are still unfamiliar skills for many fourth graders. To give your child experience in these concepts, see Measurement, page 180, and Geometry, page 169.

Question 12

To be adept at solving problems involving measurement, your child must have a strong understanding of standard units of measure and their uses. To give your child practice using standard units of measure and to help him or her develop "measurement sense," see Measurement, page 177.

Question 13

In fourth grade, children are traditionally introduced to the concepts and notation of decimals and percentages.

If you did not check A–C, your child might need additional experience working with whole numbers. See the activities in Number Sense, page 135, to reinforce these basic understandings.

If you did not check D, see Fractions, page 162.

If you did not check E, see Decimals, page 166.

If you did not check F or G, see Statistics and Probability, page 181.

Question 14

This question gives you another chance to assess your child's flexibility in using problem-solving skills.

If your child had difficulty coloring 1/4 of the circle, see Fractions, page 166.

If you did not check A–E, see Problem Solving, page 120.

If you did not check F or G, see the activities in Statistics and Probability, page 181, in addition to Problem Solving.

If you checked H, or if your child solved the problem using quick, logical reasoning, you might also want to see the activities in the Math Enrichment section, page 186.

Math curricula are not uniform around the country. It is likely that your child has been introduced to many of the concepts here but has never heard of others. If your child struggled with this assessment, talk to his or her teacher. Find out how well this assessment matches what your child is actually being taught. Ask your child's teacher if your child is working at, above, or below grade level. (The chapter titled "Working with Your Child's Teacher," page 192, might help.) If your child had little or no difficulty with the assessment, skim the book for exercises that would interest you and your child most. Feel free to adapt them in any way that is appropriate. You might also want to explore the activities in Math Enrichment, page 186. Remember that this is the time to impart the knowledge that math—discovering patterns, playing with numbers, and solving problems like a sleuth—can be joyful. Help your child to love math. Let that be your directive.

Reading Exercises

Reading Comprehension

The ability to comprehend what is read is measured by questions 1 through 6 and 8 on the Reading Assessment.

Ah, the fourth grade reader. Curled up with a copy of *James and the Giant Peach*. Poring over this month's issue of *Sports Illustrated for Kids*. Asking, please, please, *please* won't you buy him the boxed set of Boxcar Children books. It's hard to remember a time when he was struggling to remember the sound that the letters *ch* make. State curricula and language arts textbooks, too, assume that the time for learning basic reading skills is past. Your child is officially a reader. He is no longer learning to read, but rather "reading to learn." You might feel, with good cause, that you can now turn your thoughts to other concerns. And certainly there are plenty of concerns to turn to—long division or the history of your state, perhaps, not to mention soccer practice, music lessons, and scouting overnights.

Before you relax your guard, consider this troubling statistic. Sometime around fourth grade, as many as *one third* of all children in school stop progressing in reading. For some reason, these perfectly competent readers simply lose interest in reading. As their interest in reading flags, comprehension, vocabulary, and fluency skills stall out. In textbook-heavy junior high, these children begin to struggle, and by the beginning of high school, they are as much as four years behind their peers in their reading levels. Keeping up with the demands of secondary school becomes heartbreakingly difficult.

Theories abound explaining why this so-called "fourth grade slump" occurs. Some educators blame school curriculum. Others blame popular culture and television. Nearly all, at least in some part, point to a decrease in parental involvement with middle grade readers. Parents who were devoted to reading with their children when they were younger might be inclined, with support from their independence-seeking children, to let the habit slide as soon as their middle graders show they are capable of reading by themselves. Reading time loses its status in the family. Sports, club activities, lessons, homework—all perfectly legitimate activities—crowd out reading.

Certainly fourth grade is not a treacherous time for all readers. It is, however, a critical time for all readers. Even if your child is showing all the signs of becoming and remaining an avid reader, he has a lot of growing to do. He still needs help figuring out unfamiliar words and their meanings. He still needs help interpreting what he reads. Above all, he needs the opportunity to share what his reading means to him and how it fits in his life.

Simply put, you need to stay involved. Here are three ways you can help.

1. Read with your child daily.
2. Encourage your child to read independently.
3. Help your child strengthen his critical reading skills.

Remaining active in your child's reading life is the greatest intellectual gift you can give your child now—or ever. In fourth grade, your window of opportunity is particularly important. Don't let it slip away.

Reading with Your Child

Over the years, you have probably read lots of books to your child—from *Where's Spot?* to *Mike Mulligan and the Steam Shovel* to *Charlotte's Web*. Just the thought of reading with your child brings back fond memories of a small body snuggled up on your lap or

"What's This Word?"

Does your child have difficulty decoding words? Help her to build her repertoire of strategies. When your child comes to a word she doesn't know:

- Ask, "Which word would make sense here?"
- Suggest that she skip the word, read on, and then come back to the word. Once your child has read on, she may be able to predict what the word is based on context.
- Say, "Look at the first letters and last letters of the word." If a child is reading for meaning, she may need only the beginning and ending sounds to determine the word. This strategy is faster than sounding an entire word out.
- Ask, "Can you break the word into syllables?" Have your child "sound out" each syllable, blending the word together as she goes along.
- Provide the word if it is especially difficult and your child would otherwise become frustrated. Above all, you want to keep reading as smooth and as pleasurable as possible.

a sleepy head resting against your shoulder. What parent wouldn't want those days to last forever?

Sadly, it might now seem that those days are over. Ballet lessons, overdue reports on Australia, sleepovers with friends, your child's own sense of privacy and independence—all seem to conspire to keep you and your child from the shared reading time you once held so dear.

You *can* keep reading with your child. However, you may need to be more creative about finding the time and more flexible about your choice of reading material than you once were. Here's how you can do it.

HAVE FIVE MINUTES?

> ➤ Assume that your child will do some of the reading. One of the delights of having an independent reader in the house is that you can truly *share* reading. If your throat is feeling scratchy, he can take over. If he's stumbling over a particularly difficult passage, you can take over. Reading is no longer what one of you does for the other. It's a joy that you share between you.

> ➤ Take a fresh look at your daily schedule. Bedtime reading—that blessed ritual—might no longer make sense. Homework or outside activities might have begun to encroach on the time, or perhaps your child views the precious moments before sleep as his only private reading time in the day and, much as he likes reading with you, he really doesn't want to give it up. Talk to your child about establishing a new time or system for reading—perhaps right after school while he's having a snack or before he gets out of bed in the morning while you have your morning coffee. Remember, in order for reading together to become a daily habit, it must be enjoyable *for both of you.* Choose a time that makes sense.

> ➤ Read every day, even if it is only for five minutes. Many of the books your child will want to read this year will be too long to read in one sitting. "Okay," you might say. "Then we'll read a chapter a night, or fifteen minutes a night, come hell or high water." But in reality, maintaining such a rigid schedule is not always practical. So what happens when you've been up watching the fireworks and there's no way either one of you is going to make it through an entire chapter? You skip a night. Or two. Or

Block That Urge

Once your child has begun to exhibit a number of strategies, stop yourself from jumping in. If she mispronounces a word, remain silent. Again, remember that substitutions are normal. If she substitutes a word that does not make sense, it is better to give her time to self-correct. Let her know that all readers come to words they don't know, even adult readers. And that sometimes we simply guess the meaning of the word and go on.

three. Most adults know the frustration of putting down a novel and not picking it up for a few days. They lose their place. For children, the loss is even greater. Children, like adults, have other things to think about and quickly lose track of the threads of the story. Moreover, they forget why they ever liked that story in the first place. It only takes five minutes—not half an hour or a whole chapter—to keep a story alive in your child's imagination. Before you collapse from an overdose of fireworks, read for just five minutes—and keep the story alive for another day.

Picture book gems for older children might be hard to find. In bookstores and libraries they are often lumped into categories called "Picture Books" or "Children's Books." A particularly astute bookseller or librarian might be able to guide you to specific books that will thrill your fourth grader. Or you might try one of these:

- *The Faithful Friend,* by Robert D. San Souci (Simon and Schuster)
- *The Gardener,* by Sarah Stewart (Farrar, Straus and Giroux)
- *Golem,* by David Wisniewski (Clarion)
- *Grandfather's Journey,* by Allen Say (Houghton Mifflin)
- *Potato: A Tale from the Great Depression,* by Kate Lied (National Geographic)
- *Saint George and the Dragon,* by Margaret Hodges (Little, Brown)
- *The Shrinking of Treehorn,* by Florence Parry Heide (Holiday House)
- *Swamp Angel,* by Anne Isaacs (Dutton)
- *The Whingdingdilly,* by Bill Peet (Houghton Mifflin)
- *Working Cotton,* by Sherley Anne Williams (Voyager)

➤ Don't put away the picture books. Perhaps your child has been reading chapter books for a couple of years now, and you both might feel that picture books are a thing of the past. Not true. Many of your child's favorite picture books—*The Polar Express,* perhaps, or a wacky favorite like *Cloudy with a Chance of Meatballs*—still have the power to enchant. There is an ever-growing genre of picture books for older children—books like Chris Van Allsburg's *Jumanji* or *Birdie's Lighthouse,* by Deborah Hopkinson. The text in these books tends to be long and more complex, and although they might be lost on younger children, your fourth grader is in a prime position to love both the provocative illustrations and the more sophisticated text.

➤ Read the comics together. One strip of Calvin and Hobbes or Peanuts or Doonesbury takes far less than five minutes to read. Yet, a shared giggle over a cartoon or comic strip can bring all the enjoyment and good, hard thinking that a whole chapter of a not-so-great book might offer.

➤ Keep a Commuter Book going. Ask your child to read aloud while you commute to Scouts or swimming lessons. Books of poetry, such as Shel Silverstein's *Light in the Attic,* are perfect to keep in the car or in your pocket for a short trip or a subway ride to the soccer field. If you have a regular commute to or from your child's school or after-school program, keep an ongoing chapter book in the glove compartment or in your child's backpack to read on the way.

➤ Keep lots and lots and lots of reading material handy. Newspapers spread all over the breakfast table, magazines stacked on the back of the toilet, books under couches and cached beneath bedspreads and blankets—a reading house is not a tidy house. Books in a reading household are sometimes lost, often bedraggled, definitely not to be found in their proper place on the bookshelf. If clutter makes you feel like you're suffocating, try to strike a compromise. Perhaps you are willing to negotiate a clutter-free kitchen or living room in exchange for giving up your child's bedroom to a comic book infestation. And if you bruise a knee while climbing over a stack of books to kiss your angel good-night, remember: This child is READING!

➤ Share a magazine or newspaper article. Start with the headlines: LION BANNED FROM ZOO!; RAIDERS UPSET SPARTANS 72–68!; IS HUMAN CLONING NEXT? Then read enough to get the gist of the article. If your child wants more, go ahead and read the whole article. Or, if you happen to be making lunches at the time, have him read it to you!

➤ Use that library card. Fourth graders move from hockey to horses to Halloween horror stories with amazing speed. If your child brings home a stack of books on werewolves and decides that he really could care less about such things anymore, then take the books back. No harm done. What a great system!

HAVE MORE TIME?

➤ Introduce a variety of literature. Sure, you know you should read with him, but what if his reading palate never, ever strays from Goosebumps? Try to strike a compromise: your child's choice this time and your choice the next time. That way, you can at least provide *some* balance to your child's reading diet, and your child might just find a new series to love!

➤ Don't be afraid to abandon a book. Okay, you have struck a compromise, and now it's your turn to choose a book to read with your child. You choose a classic—*Peter Pan, Alice's Adventures in Wonderland, The Wind in the Willows*—only to find that the sentences are so long, the language so foreign, that you're both wondering when the chapter you're reading will ever end. What now?

Put away the book. The turned-around logic of *Alice in Wonderland,* the political satire of *Wind in the Willows,* the "Tao" of *Winnie the Pooh* are all ready and waiting for

Children's Magazines

The market for children's magazines has exploded in recent years. Though some of these magazines are definitely better than others (see below for some of the best), any magazine that you don't find truly offensive and that inspires your child to read is worth checking out. If your child has an enduring passion, you might look into adult special interest magazines such as *Sports Illustrated* or *Cat Fancier.* Take some time to look through the magazine together and talk about interesting articles.

- *American Girl* (800-234-1278)
- *Boy's Life* (972-580-2352)
- *Cricket* (800-827-0227)
- *Muse* (800-827-0227)
- *National Geographic World* (800-437-5521)
- *Sports Illustrated for Kids* (800-992-0196)
- *Ranger Rick* (703-790-4283)

your child to enjoy, but perhaps the time is not now. Be very willing to accept that any book—even a classic—at any given time might be a dud. Drop the book and move on. Keep trying until you find a book that truly captivates. Here are a few (classics included) you might try.

Realistic Fiction to Read Aloud

- *Bridge to Terabithia*, by Katherine Paterson (HarperTrophy)
- *Crow Boy*, by Taro Yahimo (Penguin)
- *From the Mixed-Up Files of Mrs. Basil E. Frankweiler*, by E. L. Konigsburg (Aladdin)
- *How to Eat Fried Worms*, by Thomas Rockwell (Watts)
- *The Hundred Dresses*, by Eleanor Estes (Harcourt)
- *Lily's Crossing*, by Patricia Reilly Giff (Dell)
- *M. C. Higgins, the Great*, by Virginia Hamilton (Aladdin)
- *My Side of the Mountain*, by Jean Craighead George (Dutton)
- *Philip Hall Likes Me, I Reckon Maybe*, by Bette Greene (Dial)
- *The Pushcart War*, by Jean Merrill (Harper)
- *Tales of a Fourth Grade Nothing*, by Judy Blume (Dell)
- *The Watsons Go to Birmingham*, by Christopher Paul Curtis (Delacourt)
- *Tuck Everlasting*, by Natalie Babbitt (Farrar, Straus and Giroux)
- *Where the Red Fern Grows*, by Wilson Rawls (Dell)

Fantasy to Read Aloud

- *Bearskin*, by Howard Pyle (Morrow)
- *If People Could Fly: American Black Folktales*, by Virginia Hamilton (Knopf)
- *Mrs. Frisby and the Rats of NIMH*, by Robert O'Brien (Scholastic)
- *The Dancing Fox: Arctic Folktales*, edited by John Bierhorst (Morrow)
- *The Girl Who Dreamed Only Geese and Other Tales of the Far North*, by Howard Norman (Harcourt Brace)
- *The Lion, the Witch, and the Wardrobe*, by C. S. Lewis (Macmillan)
- *The Phantom Tollbooth*, by Norton Juster (Random House)

➤ Encourage your child to read aloud to you. Your fourth grader can probably decode most of the words in most of the books he wants to read. The task before him now is to acquire the comprehension skills and fluency that will allow him to read even more challenging material. You can help by being there to clarify vocabulary and ask a few well-placed questions about meaning. Listen to this fourth grader and his father read Sterling North's classic story about a raccoon named Rascal:

> Fourth grader: *"It is true we were at war, observing hea-heat . . ."*
>
> Dad: "Here, cover up this part [*-less*]. What's the word?"
>
> Fourth grader: "Heat."
>
> Dad: [showing the *-less*]: "And this part?"
>
> Fourth grader: Less. Oh! . . . *heatless, meatless, and wheatless days, and conserving sugar. But my father and I did no baking and used almost none of our sugar rations. So I did not feel too unpatriotic when I gave Rascal his first sugar.* Huh? I don't get it."
>
> Dad: "During World War One, the government restricted the amount of certain foods and other items that people could use so that there would be enough supplies to send to the soldiers fighting in the war in Europe."

Fourth grader: "Even sugar? Whoa. Does that still happen?"

Dad: "Well, it happened again during World War Two. Gran and Gramps remember those times pretty well. We should ask them about it the next time we see them."

➤Read a pager-turner. You know the book. It's the one you pick up in the airport or the one you pack in your suitcase when you're off for a week with the relatives at holiday time. Your child loves the thrill of a good page-turner just as much as you do. Page-turners for children do exist, but they can be hard to find. See the list at right for suggestions.

"I couldn't put it down!"
Book Suggestions

- *Aliens Ate My Homework,* by Bruce Coville and Katherine Coville (Minstrel)
- *Bunnicula,* and others by Deborah and James Howe (Atheneum)
- *House with a Clock in Its Walls,* by John Bellairs (Dial)
- *The Master Puppeteer,* by Katherine Paterson (Avon)
- *Mystery on Bleecker Street,* by William Hooks (Knopf)
- *The Spook Birds,* by Eve Bunting (Whitman)
- *The Westing Game,* by Ellen Raskin (Dutton)

Encouraging Your Child to Read Independently

Over the years, academics and publishers have built careers and textbook empires on the question of how best to teach children to read. In the midst of all the debate, researchers and educators have consistently agreed on one point: to learn to read, a child must practice reading. According to one study, students who spend an hour a day reading materials of their own choosing develop reading comprehension skills at up to twice the rate of national norms. The idea seems simple enough: the more you read, the better you get at reading. Surprisingly, this basic idea rarely finds its way into actual teaching practices.

Certainly there is a lot of competition for the fourth grader's time both in school and out. The sad fact remains that if your fourth grader drops the reading habit now she may never catch up. For your child to stay enthusiastic, proud, and interested in reading, she must have time to read. No matter how wonderful the teacher or curriculum is, you can assume that your child will not get the time she needs for reading at school—there are simply too many demands placed on the school day. She must get it at home.

Safeguard your child's independent reading time. To start, make sure that everyone in your house knows that hanging out with a good book is a legitimate activity. If your child practices the piano fifteen minutes a day, why shouldn't she spend at least that long practicing her reading? Give her the time she needs to practice (at least twenty minutes a day) by establishing a regular time, limiting TV time, or simply by refraining to ask her to do something else. After all, what could be more important than reading?

And whenever possible, let your child read whatever she wants. Remember that your "junk" is your child's reading practice. Comics. Sports stories. Choose your own adventures. Even the latest gross-out series. You may question its quality, but this "junk" reading gives your child the practice she needs to develop strong comprehension skills. Unless you find your child's book choice to be truly offensive, try your best to trust her interests. The one sure way you can turn your newly independent reader into a "dropped the habit" reader is to demand that she read only what you want her to read.

HAVE FIVE MINUTES?

➤ Help your child find books she will like. Your child needs to find books that she likes and that she does not have to struggle to read. (Save the challenges for your time to read together.) Here are a few ways you can help her find the right books.

- Help your child gauge how difficult a book is. By this year, your child's decoding skills might be strong enough that the traditional "five finger" (five unknown words in a page) method might not tell you much. Instead, turn to a chapter in the middle of the book and suggest that your child read the page. Does something in the page intrigue her? Does she want to read on? If the passage is too complex or just plain uninteresting, she will probably just say no.

- Let your child revisit old favorites. Most likely, you, too, have made a return visit to a book you've known and loved. Old favorites give your child the comfort of familiar characters and plot. Repeat to yourself, "It does not matter that my child has read this book seventy-eight times, she is getting good practice."

- Let your child jump ship (or, in this case, jump book). Leaving a book unfinished is not a sin. How long does it take—a page, a chapter, fifty pages—to know that you and the book you're reading just aren't a good fit? Your fourth grader is learning to rely on her own judgment. Let her do that. (If, however, your child *never* finishes a book, it's likely that she needs help in getting involved and experiencing success. Make sure that she is not repeatedly distracted by other temptations and that she is choosing books at the appropriate level.)

➤ Give your child a good reason to read. Your fourth grader's interests are expanding all over the place. Her newfound dexterity in arts and crafts, her surprisingly sophisticated and quirky sense of humor, her very keen awareness of friends and feelings, her fascination with the wonderful oddities of the world around her—all give her great reasons to read. Try to decipher which way your child's current interests are blowing and help her find books that support and expand those interests.

➤ Let your child sink her teeth into a series. If you find yourself wondering just how many Babysitters' Club or Goosebumps books one child can possibly read, try not to fret. Even the most ardent series readers eventually move on to other fare. If you are dying for your child to read *Cheaper by the Dozen,* but she won't get her nose out of *The Pony Club,* spend fifteen minutes reading your choice aloud and then give her another fifteen to read on her own.

Series like Encyclopedia Brown, the American Girls, Little House, or the Boxcar Children are already the mainstay of most middle graders' reading diets. If your child loves series but is ready for a little variety, try suggesting one of these:

If your child is tiring of:	You might try:
The Boxcar Children	*All-of-a-Kind Family,* by Sidney Taylor (Yearling); *Children of the Green Knowe,* by Lucy Boston (Harcourt)
The American Girls	Dear America, series by various authors (Scholastic)
Ramona	*The Moffats,* by Eleanor Estes (Yearling); *Anastasia Krupnick,* by Lois Lowry (Houghton Mifflin); *Pippi Longstocking,* by Astrid Lindgrin (Penguin)
Nate the Great, Pam Janson, or Encyclopedia Brown	*The Great Brain,* by John D. Fitzgerald (Dial); *Bunnicula,* by Deborah and James Howe (Atheneum)
Misty of Chincoteague	*The Black Stallion,* by Walter Farley (Random House)
The Littles	*The Borrowers,* by Mary Norton (Harcourt); *The Indian in the Cupboard,* by Lynne Reid Banks (Doubleday)
Goosebumps	Animorphs, series by Katherine Applegate (Apple)

BOOKS THAT FIT YOUR CHILD'S INTERESTS

For the Giggler and Gamester

- *Falling Up*, by Shel Silverstein (HarperCollins)
- *Games Book of Sense and Nonsense Puzzles*, edited by Shusshan (Workingman's Press)
- *A Pocketful of Laughs: Stories, Poems, Jokes, Riddles*, edited by Joanna Cole (Doubleday)
- *Pun and Games: Jokes, Riddles, Daffynitions, Tairy Fales, Rhymes, and More Wordplay for Kids*, by Richard Lederer (Chicago Review Press)
- *Remember Betsy Floss, and Other Colonial Riddles*, by David Adler (Holiday House)
- *Revolting Rhymes*, by Roald Dahl (Knopf)

For the Sports Enthusiast

- *Baseball Fever*, by Johanna Hurwitz (Beechtree Books)
- *Baseball in the Barrios*, by Henry Horenstein (Gulliver Books)
- *The Fox Steals Home*, Dirt Bike Racer, and others by Matt Christopher (Little, Brown)
- *Lives of the Athletes: Thrills, Spills (and What the Neighbors Thought)*, by Kathleen Krull (Harcourt)
- *Sports Pages*, poetry by Arnold Adoff (Lippincott)
- *Swish*, by Bill Martin (Henry Holt)
- For individual biographies: *The Sports Stars* (Children's Press) and Grolier All-Pro Biographies (Grolier).

For the Artist

- *Going Back Home: An Artist Returns to the South*, by Michele Wood (the artist), Yoyomi Igus, and Toyomi Igus (Children's Book Press)
- *I Spy: An Alphabet in Art* (I Spy Series), by Lucy Micklethwait (Mulberry Books)
- *Just Like Me: Stories and Self-Portraits by Fourteen Artists*, edited by Tomie Arai (Children's Book Press)
- *Linnea in Monet's Garden*, by Christina Bjork (Farrar, Straus and Giroux)
- *The Nine-Ton Cat: Behind the Scenes at an Art Museum*, by Peggy Thompson and Barbara Moore (Houghton Mifflin)
- *Talking with Artists*, edited by Pat Cummings (Simon & Schuster)

For the Animal Lover and Naturalist

- *1,000 Facts About Wild Animals*, by Moira Butterfield (Kingfisher)
- *Creeps from the Deep*, by Norbert Wu and Leighton R. Taylor (Chronicle Books)
- *Horses*, by David Alderton (Dorling Kindersley). Dorling Kindersley puts out several series of books about animals. They are all highly visual and well researched.
- *Richard Orr's Nature Cross-Sections*, by Moira Butterfield (Dorling Kindersley)
- *The Most Beautiful Roof in the World: Exploring the Rainforest Canopy*, by Kathryn Lasky (Gulliver Green)
- *While a Tree Was Growing*, by Jane Bosveld (Workman)

BOOKS THAT FIT YOUR CHILD'S INTERESTS

For the Budding Scientist

- *A Drop of Water: A Book of Science and Wonder,* by Walter Wick (Scholastic)
- *Dinosaur Ghosts: The Mystery of Coelophysis,* by J. Lynett Gillette (Dial)
- *Explorabook: A Kid's Science Museum in a Book,* by John Cassidy (Klutz Press)
- *The Human Body: An Amazing Inside Look at You!,* by Steve Parker (Abrams)
- *I Want to Be an Astronaut,* and others by Stephanie Maze and Catherine O'Neill Grace (Harcourt)
- *Smithsonian Visual Timeline of Inventions,* by Richard Pratt (Dorling Kindersley)

For the Junior Historian

- *The Dead Sea Scrolls,* by Ilene Cooper (Morrow)
- *The History News: Explorers,* by Michael Johnstone (Candlewick). Others in this newspaper-format series include *The Aztec News, The Egyptian News, The Roman News,* and *The History News: Medicine.* All are guaranteed to captivate even the nonhistorian.
- *If You Traveled on the Underground Railroad,* and others by Ellen Levine (Scholastic)
- *My Backyard History Book,* by David L. Weitzman (Little, Brown)
- *Oh, Freedom!: Kids Talk About the Civil Rights Movement with the People Who Made It Happen* (Knopf)

For the Worldly Wise

- *Geography Wizardry for Kids,* by Margaret Kenda and Phyllis S. Williams (Barrons)
- *Tintin's Travel Diaries,* featuring Herge's popular cartoon character (Barrons)
- *The Atlas of Endangered Animals,* and others in the Environmental Atlas Series, by Stephen Thomas Pollock (Facts on File)
- *The Book of Where, or How to Be Naturally Geographic,* by Neill Bell (Little, Brown)
- *Material World: A Global Family Portrait,* by Peter Menzel, Sandra Eisert (photographer), Charles C. Mann, and Paul Kennedy (Random House)

For the Young Biographer

- *Gertrude Chandler Warner and the Boxcar Children,* by Mary Ellen Ellsworth (Whitman). A surefire hit for any avid Boxcar Children fan.
- *It Came from Ohio! My Life as a Writer,* by R. L. Stine and Joe Arther (Scholastic). About the author of the Goosebumps series.
- *Sky Pioneer: A Photobiography of Amelia Earhart,* by Corinne Szabo (National)
- *Boy,* by Roald Dahl (Greenwillow)
- *The Life and Death of Crazy Horse,* by Russell Freedman (Holiday)
- *Starry Messenger,* by Pieter Sis (Farrar Straus and Giroux)
- *I Am Rosa Parks,* by Rosa Parks and Jim Haskins (Dial)

➤ Make sure that your child has access to books. If you can possibly afford it, buy your child books of her own. These are the books she will pick up and read again and again. The more books your child has on her bookshelves, the greater chance she will pick one up and read it. The books you give your child needn't be expensive. A library castoff with a torn cover has just as much a chance of becoming a favorite as a gorgeous hardcover edition of a classic. Keep your eye out for cheap books. Here are a few places you might look:

- library sales
- yard sales
- book clubs (your child's school probably has order forms)
- secondhand book stores
- grandparents, doting aunts and uncles, well-meaning friends of the family

➤ Let your child be bored. It's a rainy Sunday afternoon, and your child is hanging around with nothing to do. *Don't* say, "Go read a book." But also don't say, "Here's a new computer game you can try." Leave your child to her own resources. She might choose to play solitaire, or draw, or just lie on her bed and stare at the ceiling. She might also choose to read.

➤ Talk about your own independent reading. Your latest Stephen King (or Jane Austen) and her latest R. L. Stine (or Frances Hodgson Burnett) might have a lot in common. Who knows?

HAVE MORE TIME?

➤ Be there to support her reading. Most fourth graders are adamant about their privacy. Unless you get into the habit of reading to each other (see above), you probably won't know whether your child is deeply contemplating every word she reads or is simply staring at the page. Sit with your child and read the paper, shuck the beans, or balance the checkbook as she reads her own book. But when she asks, "So what was so bad about the Depression?" stop what you're doing and take some time to talk.

➤ Ask your child to read aloud to you. You might feel that your child left that reading-aloud stage somewhere in second grade. In fact, the fluency that many fourth graders still need to achieve can only be gained through reading aloud. At the same time, getting your child to read to you might be a much more difficult proposition than in years past. If so, you might try these techniques:

- Give your child time to read through the passage silently before she reads it aloud. (Wouldn't you want to do the same thing if you were expected to read aloud in public?)
- Read a passage in a choppy, stumbling monotone. Invite your child to give you pointers on how to improve your reading.
- Read part of the story or chapter yourself, and then feign fatigue. Ask your child to read *just one page,* or even one paragraph, to give you a break.
- If you have a tape recorder, suggest that your child tape a story for a younger child or for you to listen to in your car.
- Take the part of one character while your child takes the part of another. Exaggerate your character's speech patterns, and encourage your child to do the same.
- At every opportunity, encourage your child to read to younger children. Siblings, nursery classes at church, and neighborhood children all make appreciative audiences.
- Suggest that your child and her friends read aloud to each other. Many fourth graders adore putting on plays. Jokes, trivia, and sports statistics are also great favorites for reading aloud, as are ghost stories at sleepovers. Supply an interesting assortment of books such as *Scary Stories to Tell in the Dark,* by Alvin Schwartz, or *Guinness Record Breakers,* by Karen Romano Young, and it's likely that your fourth grader and her friends will begin to read to one another without an additional nudge from you.

Strengthening Critical Reading Skills

Read these first two paragraphs of Sid Fleishman's delightful Newbery Award–winning book *The Whipping Boy:*

> The young prince was known here and there (and just about everywhere else) as Prince Brat. Not even black cats would cross his path.
>
> One night the king was holding a grand feast. Sneaking around behind the lords and ladies, Prince Brat tied their powdered wigs to the backs of their oak chairs.

Unless you know the story, a number of questions may already be forming in your mind: Who is this Prince Brat? Why won't black cats cross his path? Where is this story happening? And when? Why did Prince Brat play such a silly trick? What's going to happen next?

All readers ask themselves questions as they read, but some ask more—and better—questions than others. The type of self-questioning your child does greatly influences his ability to understand what he reads. In school, your child might be taught comprehension strategies such as sequencing or drawing conclusions. However, if your child learns these skills in isolation—by answering questions on ditto sheets rather than by thinking and talking about his current reading passion—he might never learn to use them to deepen his understanding and appreciation of what he is reading.

The questions your child should be asking himself are simple. Keep them in mind as you talk with your child about his—and your—reading.

1. Why is the author writing this? (author's purpose)
2. What's going to happen? (prediction, infer)
3. What connections do I see here? (cause and effect, comparisons and contrasts, classification)
4. What was this story about? (summarizing, sequencing, main idea and details)
5. What do I think about what I've read? (drawing conclusions, fact and opinion, synthesizing)

The best time to practice comprehension strategies with your child is when you are reading aloud with him. Encourage your child to stop whenever something you are reading needs clarification, but save your own questions for the end of the chapter or another good pausing place. All the critical thinking questions in the world won't help if your child has lost track of the story line and meaning.

Identifying the Author's Purpose

Why did Sid Fleishman write *The Whipping Boy?* To give us information about medieval times? To get us to laugh?

Knowing the author's purpose can go a long way in helping a reader to determine *how* to read (slowly with intent to learn, more quickly when the purpose is to have fun and entertain). Three of the most common reasons authors write are:

1. to inform
2. to entertain
3. to persuade

You'll want to help your child realize, however, that many times an author has more than one reason for writing. Sid Fleishman might have hoped to achieve two purposes: to entertain and to inform. As you explore these concepts, you will help your child become a wiser, more discriminating reader.

HAVE FIVE MINUTES?

➤Before your child begins reading a homework assignment, ask, "What kind of reading are you going to need to do? Will you skim the page, read quickly, or slow down and read more carefully?" A page of story problems for math class will need to be read much more slowly than a tall tale for language arts. (For specific strategies for reading nonfiction, see Study Skills, page 91.)

➤ By this time, your fourth grader should know the difference between fiction and nonfiction and is probably ready to learn about other genres. Take your child to a library or a bookstore to see how different shelves are organized. Whenever you and your child select a book to read, talk about why the author might have chosen to write in that particular genre. For instance, you might say, "I think this author chose to write poetry about water because poetry can make us stop and think about something in a different way."

➤ Use family discussions to help your child realize that the same information can be presented in different ways—depending upon the author's purpose. Invite family members to restate a single need to show different purposes. Look at how many ways a request to clean up a room can be approached:

> ## Help your child to identify these genres:
>
> - Realistic fiction (imaginary stories based on things that could really happen)
> - Fantasy (imaginary stories about things that could not really happen)
> - Historical fiction (imaginary stories based on historical events)
> - Biographies (true stories about real people)
> - Poetry (rhymes and songs)
> - Mysteries and adventures (stories built on suspense)
> - Folktales or legends (stories that have been passed along from generation to generation)

- To persuade: "Willie, if you get your room clean by dinner time, we'll probably have time to go out for pizza."
- To inform: "Willie, there are exactly three pairs of pants, five dirty socks, twenty-one baseball cards, four miscellaneous pieces of paper, and two unidentified objects on the floor of your room."
- To entertain:
  There was once a young man named Will
  Whose dirty room made us all ill.
  So we hired a man
  To take it off in his van
  And presented young Will with the bill!

HAVE MORE TIME?

➤ Choose a well-known story, such as Goldilocks and the Three Bears. Ask your child to rewrite or tell the story with a different purpose in mind.

For example, he might write a letter from the bears to Goldilocks's parents in order to *persuade* them to pay for the damage Goldilocks has done, or he might use the story to provide *information* about bears' habitats and living habits. If you are going on a long car ride, see if every person in the car can make up a Goldilocks story, each with a different purpose.

➤ Suggest that your child cut a number of different features from various sections of the newspaper. Then have him sort the articles according to whether they entertain, inform, or persuade. If your child runs into articles that have more than one purpose, help him set up a Venn diagram to show the overlap. (Articles with just one purpose are recorded in the outer circles. Articles that share two or more purposes are recorded in the sections that overlap.)

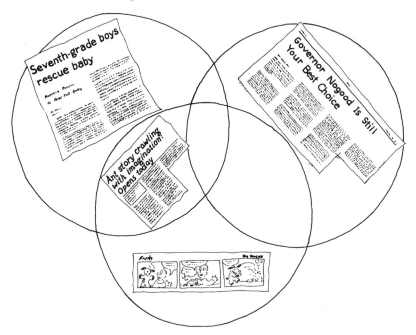

➤ Have an Author's Night. Invite each member of the family to come to dinner dressed as the author of a book each family member has read. Ask each author questions about his writing process, such as:
  • Why did you write this book?
  • What special information did you want your audience to get out of this book?
  • How did you want your audience to feel after reading this book?

Making Predictions

Your child begins to make predictions about a book before he even cracks its cover. Will it be a spine-tingler or a tender pet story? Where will the story be set? Do its characters look interesting? But there is much more to making predictions than looking at a book's cover. As your child continues to predict as he is reading (What will the character do? How will this story end?), he is developing the ability to make *inferences*—to draw on what he knows to go beyond the stated facts. Making and revising and confirming predictions is what keeps reading active. Fourth graders use context to predict what words say and mean, they use chapter headings and picture captions to predict the action of the story, and they use their own understanding of the story to predict what will happen next.

HAVE FIVE MINUTES?

➤ As you stand with your child at the library checkout desk, or when you take a moment to find the chapter you left off reading last night, ask your child to make some predictions. What do you think this book is about? What will the characters do? How on earth are they ever going to solve this problem? And after the book has been read: Were your predictions right?

➤ If you are watching TV, take time during the commercials to make predictions about how the show is going to end. Write your predictions on note cards and save them until the end of the show. The person whose prediction was most accurate gets fifteen extra minutes of reading time.

➤ While standing in line at the grocery store, ask your child to check out the headlines on the cover of a newspaper or magazine and predict what the stories might be about.

➤ Use the prediction "leg-ups" that nonfiction books often provide. After your child has checked the cover and illustrations, point out the table of contents, chapter headings, and subheads if they exist.

➤ When reading or listening to a news report, ask your child to predict what the next day's article on the same subject will say. Don't forget to talk about why he made the predictions he did.

➤ Most children are pretty astute at using small clues to predict outcomes in family life. For example, in some families a "We'll see" response to a child's request means no. In other families, it means probably or yes. Talk about the predictions your child makes on a daily basis. A tucked-away vase's sudden appearance on the table might always mean that Great-Aunt Mildred is coming for a visit.

HAVE MORE TIME?

➤ Play Out of Context. At the library, or anywhere there is unfamiliar reading material handy, pick up a book and read a few paragraphs from the middle of it. Invite your child to tell you what the beginning and the ending of the story might be about.

➤ Tear a page from a catalog, a take-out menu, or your child's cast-off comic book in half. Then challenge your child to complete the lines of text by figuring out what the missing portions say. Encourage your child to go for the sense of text rather than a word-for-word match up.

➤ Good mysteries are chock-full of opportunities for predicting outcomes. Read a mystery together (see the list of page turners on page 65) and suggest that your child draw a simple chart or diagram to keep track of the clues and predictions.

Recognizing Additional Connections (cause and effect, compare and contrast, classification)

Good comprehension depends upon the ability to make connections. What are the causes and effects of a character's actions? In *The Lion, the Witch, and the Wardrobe,* what were the consequences of Edmund's returning to Narnia? What do you learn when you compare and contrast settings, plots, events, and characters? How are Lucy and Edmund the same? How are they different? How would you classify the story elements? Would you classify Edmund as a friend or an enemy of Aslan? Helping your child think about connections as she reads will strengthen her ability to understand the meaning of what she reads.

HAVE FIVE MINUTES?

➤ Talk about the causes and effects of everyday occurrences, from the whimsical ("I wonder how that banana sticker got stuck on your back?") to the practical ("Why do you think Aunt Carol called?") to the downright disastrous ("What would happen if an earthquake struck right now?").

➤ Ask your child "what-if" questions, such as:
  • What if the garbage collectors went on strike?
  • What if you're a guest at someone's house and you don't like what's for dinner?

- What if you always knew what was going to happen next?

Don't forget that each of the effects imagined might cause other effects. For instance, garbage piling shoulder-high on the sidewalk might attract an overabundance of wildlife.

➤ Play Double Categories. You probably remember filling time years ago by asking your child to name all the farm animals he could think of. Stretch the activity by asking your child to name things that fit two categories at once; for example, "things made of glass" and "things that roll" (marble, test tube, drinking glass).

HAVE MORE TIME?

➤ Ask your child to write on index cards the titles of ten books he has recently read. Then suggest that he sort the cards in any way he wants. Talk about his choices: perhaps several of the books had characters in common, or maybe some were historical novels while others were lists of strange-but-true-facts. After he has classified the titles, challenge him to find a new way to sort them.

➤ Be sure your child knows how to make and use a Venn diagram. Use the diagram to compare settings, characters, events, or ideas.

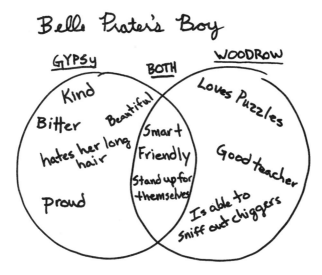

➤ Suggest that your child devise a way to organize his private collection of books or magazines other than alphabetizing. He might wish to create labels for shelves or decorate large cardboard boxes for each type of book.

➤ Talk about the physics of cooking while you bake or prepare meals. How are baking soda and baking powder alike? How are they different? What makes a soufflé rise (or fall)? What would happen if you put a baking potato in a microwave without piercing it first? If the cook in your house doesn't know all the answers (and who does?), try one of these books:

- *Cooking Wizardry for Kids,* by Margaret Kenda and Phyllis Williams (Barrons)
- *The Science Chef,* by Joan D'Amico and Karen Eich Drummond (John Wiley and Sons)
- *Science Experiments You Can Eat,* by Vicki Cobbs (Harper)
- *Soda Science: Designing and Testing Soft Drinks,* Boston Children's Museum (Morrow)

➤ Read several versions of the same story. Comparing and contrasting variations of an old favorite can be both enlightening and great fun. For example, try these versions of good old Cinderella:

- *Cinderella,* retold by Marcia Brown (Macmillan)
- *Ella Enchanted,* by Carson Levine (HarperCollins)
- *The Korean Cinderella,* by Shirley Climo (HarperCollins)
- *Moss Gown,* by William Hooks (Clarion)
- *Mufaro's Beautiful Daughters: An African Tale,* by John Steptoe (Lothrop, Lee, and Shephard)
- *Prince Cinders,* by Babette Cole (Putnam)
- *Vasilissa the Beautiful,* by Elizabeth Winthrop (HarperCollins)

➤ Teach your child how analogies work. Then suggest that he make up some of his own to challenge you.

- Michael Jordan is to basketball as ___ is to figure skating.
- Noisy is to the school bus as quiet is to the ___.
- 25¢ is to $1.00 as ___ is to 1 hour.

Summarizing and Sequencing

"And then . . . and then . . . and then . . ." Sound familiar? It's your fourth grader telling you about something that happened in school today, or recounting the plot of the latest Babysitters' Club book, or giving you a blow-by-blow description of how she saved the world from destruction in her computer game. On the one hand, fourth graders make great summarizers. Their almost fanatic attention to detail gives them powers of observation and analysis that seemed far out of reach just a year ago. On the other hand, it sometimes seems that they just don't know where to stop. Helping your fourth grader learn to summarize, to distinguish between main ideas and details, and to arrange events in sequence will strengthen her reading as well as her writing and thinking.

➤ Your fourth grader is probably doing a lot of reading without you these days. Even if you are devoted to bedtime reading, you probably get no farther than the end of a chapter or a number of pages each night. Make a deal with your child. You will ignore that flashlight shining from under the covers if she promises you that she will catch you up on what's been happening in the book that she's "secretly" been reading there.

➤ As you read or watch television together, jot down events from the program on index cards or strips of paper. Later, mix the cards and challenge your child to put them in the order of occurrence.

➤ Sharing information about the events of the day is probably the most consistent practice your child will ever get in summarizing. Too often, however, the summary goes something like this: "What'd ya do at school today?" "Nothin'." Questions like these might help your child focus on the main event or interesting details.
  • What was the one best thing that happened today?
  • What was one thing you did well today?
  • If your day were a book, what would its title be? (Not *The Day Nothin' Happened!*)
  • If your day were a movie, who would have starred in it?
  • What was one thing that pulled you up (made you feel good about yourself)? Was there anything that pulled you down?

➤ Encourage your child to use the story maps in the back of the book (page 217) to keep track of the sequence, main idea, and details of stories she has read.

➤ Give your child instructions in an incorrect order. See how long it takes her to catch your mistake.

➤ Play Headlines by the Book. Make up a headline based on the plot of a familiar book. See if your child can name the book and then make up another headline to stump you. Here are a couple to get you started.
  • GIRL STRANDED ON DESERTED ISLAND! (*Island of the Blue Dolphins*)
  • BOY DISCOVERS ENORMOUS FRUIT! (*James and the Giant Peach*)

HAVE MORE TIME?

➤ Encourage your child to plan a science experiment. Planning an experiment entails coming up with a main idea (for example, "Does listening to music affect how well I do on my math homework?"), deciding on a sequence of steps ("I'll listen to music while I do my homework this week and won't listen to music next week"), and noting details ("Was the first week's homework easier anyway?")

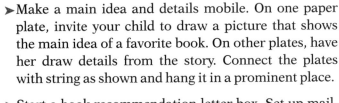

➤ Make a main idea and details mobile. On one paper plate, invite your child to draw a picture that shows the main idea of a favorite book. On other plates, have her draw details from the story. Connect the plates with string as shown and hang it in a prominent place.

➤ Start a book recommendation letter box. Set up mailboxes or cubbies in your house and create postcards or telegram forms out of index cards. Encourage family members to write *brief* summaries of books they think others would like and "mail" them to the appropriate people. If your child likes this activity, she might want to mail real postcard recommendations to friends.

➤ If your child is having difficulty keeping track of the sequence of events or details in a book, show her how to make a book square. She can keep the square in her book as a bookmark and add information to it as she reads.

HOW TO MAKE A BOOK SQUARE

1. Cut a 8 1/2" square out of notebook or printer paper (plain white paper is best).
2. Fold the paper into fourths and open it. Then fold in each corner toward the center.
3. If working on sequence, write the numbers 1 through 4 on the outside of the flaps. If working on details, write WHO, WHAT, WHEN, WHERE.
4. On the underside of each flap, write the appropriate event or detail.
5. Open the square. In the center, write the title of the book and a sentence describing the main idea of the book.

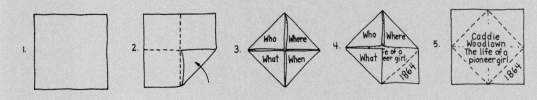

➤You know that drawer full of photographs you've been meaning to do something with? Hand the task to your fourth grader. Buy or make albums or photo boxes and ask your child to organize the photos in chronological order and caption them.

Drawing Conclusions

Drawing conclusions is a life skill. You draw conclusions from your own experience, from what you know has already happened, from what, logically, you think might happen. If your mechanic says your car has about 10,000 miles to go before it just gives up, do you fix it or buy a new car? Your conclusion depends on the information you have been given and what you already know. In order to understand why story characters do the things they do, or why historical events occurred, or why an answer to a math problem is a reasonable solution, your fourth grader needs to be able to draw conclusions.

HAVE FIVE MINUTES?

➤After your child has finished a book, ask her questions that encourage her to draw conclusions. Remember to accept her responses with appreciation and respect. The more you encourage your child to express her opinions, the more thoughtful her opinions will become.
  • Which book did you like better, *Sounder* or *Shiloh*? Why?
  • If you had been the dog's owner, what would you have done?
  • Did you like the ending? What would you change about it?
  • Would I like that book?

➤Do your very best to let your child draw her own conclusions about everyday life. Why is there a sudden glut of Beanie Babies on the market? Why did Sarah decide to go swimming with Jodi instead of with me?

➤Differentiate between facts and opinions. (A statement of fact can be proven true or false; a statement of opinion cannot be proven.) Point out advertisements, billboards, and statements in the newspaper and say, "Is this fact or opinion?" You will be surprised at how gray the lines can get, but also at how astute your fourth grader can be in her reasoning process. Deciphering fact from opinion only gets harder as the world gets more complex. Any time you spend on this skill now will help your child make her way through the world at large in the future.

➤When your kids are squabbling in the back seat of the car, shout, "Okay, FACT: This car is not going another mile farther with squabbling kids in the backseat!" Is it fact or opinion? Before your kids can test you, hit them with another one: "Okay, FACT: This fellow in England wrecked 2,003 cars and all because of squabbling children." Fact or opinion? By now you should have them interested, and you can look up any dubious facts when you get to the nearest library. (Yes, Dick Sheppard of Gloucester, England, wrecked 2,003 cars, but not because of squabbling children.)

➤ Invite your child to pick a photograph from a book, magazine, or newspaper. Then ask your child to give you as much information as she can based on what she sees in the picture. If you can—and it might take a while—make an effort to substantiate the information.

➤ Challenge your child to come up with a list of people who use the skill of drawing conclusions in their careers: doctors and nurses (based on symptoms and tests), weather forecasters (based on atmospheric conditions), police detectives (based on evidence). Talk about your days: When did you find yourself drawing conclusions? Were the conclusions based on reliable information? If not, what were they based on?

➤ Cut a favorite comic strip out of the newspaper. Then cut off the last box. Ask your child to draw the conclusion to the comic strip.

➤ Play the game of Because. Say "Isabelle chose to wear her skirt on backward today because—" or "I'm afraid we have no bread today because—." or Invite your children to draw their own conclusions—the sillier the better.

➤ Play There's No Place Like Home. List three to six clues. If your child guesses where "home" is, she gets to give the next set of clues.
  • It's warm there all year-round.
  • Grammy and Pops live near there.
  • It reminds me of Disney World.
    (Orlando, Florida)
  or
  • It's the favorite place of a raccoon.
  • It is found deep in a forest.
  • Lots of bugs make their home there as well.
    (A hole in a tree.)
  A variation of this game is There's No One Like Me! The goal of this game is to guess the identity of a person.

➤ Talk about improbables. Why do your knees bend out instead of in? Why is ice sometimes blue? Why do people continue to learn long division? Any ideas? Ask your child to come up with some conclusions of her own.

If you need more ideas, see if you can find *Do Penguins Have Knees?*, *Why Do Clocks Run Clockwise?*, and other "imponderables" by David Feldman. (Or, as one ten-year-old was heard to say, "Why are they called imponderables if you ponder them?")

HAVE MORE TIME?

➤ Tell or read fables, and ask your child to come up with the morals. If you need help coming up with the stories, there are many fables available both in collections and in picture book form. (See box for suggestions.)

Check Out These Fables Old and New

- *Aesop's Fables*, selected by S. A. Handsford (Puffin)
- *Doctor Coyote: A Native American Aesop's Fables*, by John Bierhorst (Macmillan)
- *Fables*, by Arnold Lobel (Harper & Row)
- *The Rabbit's Judgment*, by Suzanne Crowder Han (Henry Holt)
- *Yo Aesop! Get a Load of These Fables*, by Paul Rosenthal (Simon & Schuster)

➤ Invite your child to draw places or people from her favorite book. What does the Secret Garden look like? How about Willie Wonka's Chocolate Factory? What about the Great Gilly Hopkins, or M. C. Higgins, the Great? When you invite your child to draw her impressions, you are literally asking her to draw conclusions. It's not as easy as you think—try it yourself!

➤ Play Charades. It's a perfect game for fourth graders' flair for drama, and it's great for reinforcing the skill of drawing conclusions. You can play informally with one person trying to stump the rest of the family, or you can play by official team rules. Use familiar book titles or characters (including animals, of course). Your fourth grader will love it, and in spite of yourself, so will you.

➤ Play strategy games, such as Chess. Strategy games usually require players to use information to draw conclusions and predict results—the same higher-level thinking skills that make a proficient reader. For a list of strategy games appropriate for fourth graders, see Finding the Fun in Mathematics, page 121.

Vocabulary

The ability to recognize vocabulary words is measured by questions 3 and 5 on the Reading Assessment.

What makes one fourth grader fly through reading practically anything he can get his hands on, and another child slip into boredom and disinterest? In a word—vocabulary. Those 3,000 words your child needed to know by the end of third grade have done him well so far. But those 3,000 (as compared to the 120,000 proficient adult readers recognize) can hardly stand up to the likes of *The Wolves of Willoughby Chase* (Joan Aiken) or *The Moorchild* (Eloise McGraw). Reading for reading's sake is no fun. Reading is only fun when the words catch the imagination, when they connect to open new worlds and thoughts. For this to happen, your child must know what the words *mean*.

In many fourth grades, vocabulary instruction is a big deal. Your child will undoubtedly be encountering new words, specific to his study, throughout the year. If you are aware of your child's vocabulary lists (sometimes new vocabulary words show up on spelling lists) as you and your child read together, you can briefly point words out and talk about how they add to the meaning of what you are reading. There is simply no better way to build vocabulary skills than to read and to talk. No workbooks or flash cards will give your child the adequate practice he needs to figure out what an unfamiliar word means.

Antonyms and Synonyms

Antonyms are easy. Your child has been figuring out "what's the opposite of *good*" ever since he was in preschool. Synonyms, on the other hand, are slippery. Synonyms (look in any thesaurus) mean *almost* the same as another word. *Happy, kind, proper, awesome,* and even *tasty* can all be synonyms for the word *good.*

Homonyms (Homophones)

These are words that sound the same but are spelled differently and have different meanings. *Dear* and *deer* are homonyms, as are *to, two,* and *too.* Readers generally use context clues to figure out the meaning of homonyms as they read. Writers, on the other hand, have a much more difficult task—they must match up the meaning of the word with its (it's?) correct spelling.

Words with Multiple Meanings (Homographs)

Many—if not most—words have multiple meanings. ("Can you do the can-can on a can?") Most fourth graders don't have any difficulty figuring out whether *can* means "is able to" or "a metal container." The problem comes when words are spelled the same but are pronounced differently *and* have different meanings. These words, such as *tear* (a tear in your eye) and *tear* (a tear in a piece of fabric) can wreak havoc for the fourth grade reader.

Figurative Language

Figurative language that is used to set up a comparison between two seemingly unlike things is the spice of reading and writing. Figurative language can be easy to recognize in poetry, as in these famous lines from Carl Sandburg:

> The fog comes
> on little cat feet.

But figurative language can be highly troublesome for the fourth grader who is just trying to "get the words right." Although fourth graders are beginning to recognize figurative language in reading, they should not be expected to use it in their writing.

- *Similes* use the words *like* or *as* to compare: The fog is *as* soft *as* cats' feet.
- *Metaphors* do not use *like* or *as* to compare: "The fog comes on little cat feet."
- *Onomatopoeia* refers to words that imitate sounds: *buzz, murmur, swoosh.*

Idioms, Puns, and Exaggerations (Hyperbole)

Most fourth graders adore the playfulness of idiomatic language ("I'm going to turn over a new leaf and get my tree project done early. Get it? Turn over a new leaf?"). And are experts at hyperbole ("This has been the worst day of my whole entire life!"). Still, even good readers can be stumped by phrases such as "eat your heart out" or "keep your head above water."

You cannot instill in your child a love of words any more than you can instill a love of numbers or of broccoli. What you *can* do is find ways to show your fourth grader how much fun playing around with words can be. When your child looks upon the quirks and puzzles of words as a game, learning new vocabulary and exploring its vagaries are just plain fun. In the process, you will be strengthening his vocabulary skills and giving him the tools he needs to glide over the potential reading snags in fourth grade.

HAVE FIVE MINUTES?

➤ Read aloud. Your child's listening comprehension level can be up to *three times* his independent reading level. The stories you read to your child are therefore far richer in vocabulary than the books he reads on his own. The conversations you have together while reading give your child a chance to double-check words he doesn't know and a chance to talk about such oddities of the English language as homonyms, idioms, and figurative patterns of speech.

➤ *Polyglot.* Now there's a word! Find some fun words in written material or while listening to a television or radio show, and talk about them. Talk about word parts: "What do you think *poly-* means? What's a *polygon*?" If possible, piece together the parts: if *poly* means "many" and *glot* means "languages," what does *polyglot* mean? You can use a dictionary to help you.

Dictionaries both new and used can be inexpensive and are easily obtained (see Study Skills on page 91). Collect a few and scatter them around the house. They'll be readily available the next time you want to conduct word surgery.

➤ Use big words in conversation. Don't worry if the word you use isn't exactly the one you had in mind. Misusing words is a natural part of childhood—you probably have a few fond memories of your own child's insisting that certain arctic creatures are called "polo bears." Now that your child is older, she may be less inclined to take such risks and therefore, unwittingly, may be limiting her own vocabulary. Show her that taking risks can actually be fun. Don't hesitate to use a word you're not quite sure of. Pause and say, "*Amorphosize.* Is that a word?" Look it up and giggle over your own mistakes. Mistakes in vocabulary even have a name: malapropisms (after the eighteenth-century playwright Sheridan's character named Mrs. Malaprop, who was inclined to say such things as "He is the very pineapple of politeness!"). The point here is to risk, to correct, and to have fun.

➤ Encourage your child over and over and over again to tell you what's exciting her or what's bugging her—in new ways, in different ways, with new words:

"I hate Kayla Thurgood!"

"You what?"

"I hate her!"

"Um, I'm not quite clear on this. Can you say it another way?"

"I detest her! She makes me sick! She always gets other people in trouble! I can't stand the way she squiggles around in her seat and snuffles and everything when I'm just trying to do my math!"

The emotions this fourth grader is dealing with are clearly intense—and wow, what a great vocabulary! Sometimes, the more ways you can state a problem, the easier that problem is to solve.

➤ Use synonyms in your daily talk. If your fourth grader tells you that homework is hard, reflect back what she said using another word for *hard.* Your conversation might go something like this:

"This homework is hard."

"Yep, I bet it's pretty tedious."

Slowly, but surely, your child's vocabulary will grow.

➤ Stamp out squishy words. *Went, was, nice, good*—all are squishy words that, because their meaning is not very specific or because they're overused (especially by fourth graders), have nearly lost their meaning. Get into the habit of giving the evil eye whenever you hear "And then she went—and then I went—" or "It was so cool!" Ask for one—just one— more specific word ("It was so *scary*!") and stretch that vocabulary. Although squishy words do come in handy now and then, they don't do much to help the fourth grader who's trying to expand her vocabulary.

➤ While walking to the corner drugstore or to the subway, challenge your child to come up with as many synonyms as she can for the word *walk.* If you have a scrap of paper and pencil handy, make a list. Do the same for *said* or *made.* At home, collect your lists and start your own thesaurus.

➤ How many figures of speech can you think of that use the word *throw*? (throw in the towel, throw a party, throw a fit) How about *play*? See how long a list you and your child can make.

➤ At the bank, in a restaurant, or waiting for the bus, make up a Quick List. Start with a category such as "ugly words" or "musical words" or "words that have five syllables." See how many words you can come up with before you are shown to your table or the bus comes. Here are some possible Quick List ideas:

• Words that mean "eat"
• Antonyms (opposites)
• Soothing words
• Words that have two (or more) meanings
• Words that have to do with computers

HAVE MORE TIME?

➤ Develop a family crossword puzzle habit. If one of your family members spends a good portion of Sunday afternoon working the crossword puzzle in the Sunday paper, so much the better. Just make sure that your child is included in figuring out some of the words. If you're sitting in an airport and your plane has been delayed, ask your child to construct a crossword puzzle on the back of your ticket folder.

➤ Play Charades. Write words (your child's weekly spelling list, if he has one, or a list of words connected with something you're doing at home) on slips of paper. Take turns acting out and guessing the words.

➤ Standing in the checkout line at the grocery store, start a simile chain. See how many comparisons you can come up with.
  - As hungry as a . . .
  - As bored as a . . .
  - As wiggly as a . . .
  - As slow as a . . .
  - As silly as a . . .

Word Play

Check in your library or bookstore for books that play with words.

- *A Cache of Jewels, and Other Collective Nouns,* and others by Ruth Heller (Grosset and Dunlap)
- *cdb!* and *cdc!,* by William Steig (Simon and Schuster)
- *Easy as Pie: A Guessing Game of Sayings,* by Marcia Folsom and Michael Folsom (Clarion)
- *Eight Ate: A Feast of Homonym Riddles,* by Marvin Terban (Clarion)
- *Mad as a Wet Hen!: And Other Funny Idioms,* by Marvin Terban (Clairon)
- *What's a Frank Frank?: Tasty Homograph Riddles,* by Giuilo Maestro (Clarion)
- *What's in a Word?: A Dictionary of Daffy Definitions,* by Rosale Moscovitch (Houghton Mifflin)

➤ Broaden your child's understanding of words and their specific uses by participating in new experiences. Walk in the woods, play baseball, listen to music. If you find yourself taking your family to the first curling match of your (or any of your ancestors') lives, ask questions. What is a broom? Is it the same tool you use to sweep the floor?

➤ Declare a Backwards Day. On Backwards Day, everyone must speak in opposites (antonyms)—but without using the words *not* or *no* or a contraction containing *n't* such as *don't* or *isn't.* For example, when it's time to call your children to breakfast, you might have to say, "Kids, *go up*stairs for *dinner!*" The resulting chaos will delight your fourth grader. It might make for a confusing day, but you can rest assured that your child will listen hard (not necessarily a bad attribute for a fourth grader!) and respond in kind—and will get some practice in recognizing antonyms in the process!

➤ Play word games (see Spelling, page 111). Most word games have more to do with spelling than meaning, but in the course of playing the game, meaning does crop up. For instance, every time your child challenges you in Scrabble, and you look up a word, you introduce a new definition.

➤ Play Pictionary. The commercial games Pictionary and Pictionary Junior make great gifts for fourth graders. Look at a few simple cards in each and decide which best suits your own fourth grader's skills. You can also play a homemade version by taking turns drawing a picture of a word. If your child guesses the word, you each get a point. If you reach a certain number of points, you both get a treat.

➤ Create a pun wall. Explain to your fourth grader that puns are a play on words—particularly words that have more than one meaning. Hang up a sheet of paper and invite the family to disfigure it to their hearts' content with graffiti—but with one requirement. The graffiti must contain a pun.

Word Study

The ability to analyze words is measured by questions 1, 3, and 5 on the Reading Assessment.

By fourth grade, your child should know that the sounds of *c-a-t* blend together to make *cat* or that *sh-ar-p* makes *sharp*. Beyond these simple phonics (letter and sound combinations), she has probably come to realize that many words contain spelling patterns that make predictable sounds, as the pattern *oi* does in *noisy, boil,* and *rejoice.* By fourth grade, even the most rigid phonics-based reading programs have moved away from letter sounds toward what is generally called "word study" or "structural analysis." Unlike phonics, word study starts with the whole word and moves to its parts—its syllables, its prefixes and suffixes, and its "add-ons" (officially called inflections). If approached in an informal manner, word study consists of little more than playing with words—taking them apart and putting them back together again. This "play" is vitally important. You can help your child learn English, not by drilling her on prefixes and suffixes but by showing her the logic behind even this most illogical language and just how marvelous words can be.

HAVE FIVE MINUTES?

➤ Whenever you or your child comes across an unfamiliar name or a long word (*nationwide*, for example), model breaking the word into syllables to figure it out. Put your finger over all but the first syllable and read that syllable (*na-*). Then move your fingers so that only the first two syllables show, and blend the two syllables together (*na-tion*). Continue until you've sounded out the entire word.

➤ Hop, skip, sing, or clap syllables. The more practice your child has in recognizing syllables, the easier both reading and spelling will be for her.

➤ What month is it? January? May? September? Have your child create a menu for the month, but here's the rub: each of the dishes must have the same number of syllables as the month itself.

➤ Got a train, plane, or car trip ahead? Start a compound word chain—a list of words in which each new word uses the second part of the word just ahead of it. Begin with an easy compound word such as *outside*. Another person then comes up with *sidewalk*. Next comes *walkman*. Then *manhole*. See how long you can make your chain.

➤ Build words. Start with the word *friend*. Take turns adding prefixes and suffixes to the word to create new words, such as *friendly, friendship, befriend, unfriendly*. Talk about how each word part changes the meaning of the word. Other base words you might use are *love* (*unlovable, lovely, beloved, lovelorn*) or *sense* (*nonsense, sensible, senseless, sensibility*).

➤ Ask "If *tri-* means *three*, what's a triangle? How about a tricycle? How about a tricorn hat?"

HAVE MORE TIME?

➤ Play Word Scavenger Hunt. Have your child choose a page from a favorite book, comic, or newspaper section and estimate how many words ending in *-er* (or any other word part she is currently studying) she can find. Have her find the words. How close did she come to the estimate?

➤ Play Cat. The object of the game is to form as many words as possible that contain *cat*. Don't say the actual words, but give each other clues, such as:
  • This cat is a disaster (*catastrophe*).
  • This cat becomes a butterfly (*caterpillar*).
  • This cat lists things you can buy (*catalog*).

Challenge your child to come up with other small words that form a part of larger words, such as *age, can,* or *ape.*

Study Skills

The ability to use study skills is measured by questions 6 and 7 on the Reading Assessment.

Life used to be so easy. Your child went to school, spent the day reading, writing, and doing 'rithmetic, and came home. His backpack was stuffed with stories and drawings and maybe a math worksheet here or there. Perhaps in third grade things got a little more serious—spelling words to study by Friday, or a composition due each week. But fourth grade—well, that's *serious.*

Suddenly, reading, writing, and 'rithmetic aren't all there is anymore. There's a science textbook to keep track of now, and those handouts from health class, and that report on Ellis Island that's due tomorrow . . . or was it today? How did life get so complicated so quickly?

Your child is facing new challenges, in content as well as in expectations. But that doesn't mean he is ill equipped for the task. He has spent three—possibly even more—years building basic reading skills and strategies. Now all he needs to do is learn how to apply them. Here are some ways you can help:

- By helping your child locate the information he needs.
- By helping your child learn to use dictionaries and information resources.
- By helping your child organize information effectively.
- By helping your child learn to give oral presentations.

Locating Information

Chances are, your child is already familiar with your local library. Perhaps he remembers attending story hours there as a toddler, perusing the picture book section as a beginning reader, or picking out his own chapter books as his reading improved and he gained independence. Now it's time to broaden his horizons even further. Visit your library often, and take a few extra minutes to explore its nooks and crannies. By teaching your child how to find his way around the library and how to ask for help, you are giving him valuable skills that he will use not only throughout his academic career but throughout his life.

HAVE FIVE MINUTES?

➤ Take a quick tour of your library. Where is the fiction located? How about nonfiction? How about CDs, videos, newspapers, and magazines? Where is the reference section? The card catalog?

➤ Make sure your child knows how to find a book. Most libraries now have computerized catalog systems. Show your child how to look up books by author, title, or subject, and how to limit his search by being as specific as possible. Suggest that he search for his current passion—say, "diseases"—and see how many entries show up. Then try a more specific topic, such as "the plague," and note how much more efficient the search becomes.

➤ Introduce your child to your library's classification system (Dewey Decimal or Library of Congress) and then enlist his help in finding books for family members.

➤ Most fourth graders are mesmerized by facts, and there's no greater depository of facts, records, and miscellaneous information than the reference section of the library. Be sure to give your little fact-finder ample time to explore such wonders as
  • *The Guinness Book of World Records*
  • *The World Almanac*
  • *Famous First Facts*
  • *The Book of Lists*
  • *American Averages*
  • *Consumer Reports Yearbook*

HAVE MORE TIME?

➤ Go on a library scavenger hunt. With your child, make a list of questions such as the ones listed below. Work together to see how quickly you can find the answer to each of the questions.
  • What happened on this day 100 years ago?
  • Who is the oldest person in the world?
  • How many books by Roald Dahl are in this library?
  • What call numbers would you look under if you wanted a book about insects?

➤ Invite your child to make a bookmark that lists the Dewey Decimal or Library of Congress classifications (depending upon which system your local library uses). Encourage him to illustrate the different sections for easy reference when he goes to the library.

Using Dictionaries and Other Information Resources

So, your fourth grader has found the book she needs. What now? Most teachers assume that fourth graders know how to find words and topics in alphabetical order in dictionaries and encyclopedias. This year, your child will probably expand upon that basic knowledge—for example, to use "See also" references to find additional information. In the course of her content-area research, she will also probably learn how to use the different parts of a nonfiction book (index, table of contents, glossary, appendices) to locate information.

HAVE FIVE MINUTES?

➤ Look it up. Who was Harry Houdini? When did the Berlin Wall fall? Is a platypus a mammal? Even if answering your child's difficult questions is good for your ego, *not* answering is better for your child. Scratch your head, look perplexed, and say, "Hmmm. I wonder where we can find the answer?" Keep a list of stumpers on the door of the refrigerator. Then go to the library, use the Internet, or check out reference books you have at home.

➤ Make sure your child knows how to use guide words. In order to be able to use almost any reference material efficiently, your child must have the skill of alphabetizing down pat. Make sure your child can alphabetize to the third or fourth letter. If your child seems to be having difficulty with this concept, write words (grocery lists and guest lists work well) on slips of paper and have her place them in alphabetical order.

➤ Encourage your child to pick out and read nonfiction books. Fourth graders are great investigators and love to delve deeply into a subject if given the chance. Follow your child's passions. As you explore nonfiction books with your child, ask questions such as "Does this book have a chapter on Jane Goodall?" "Where was that information on how gorillas communicate?" and "What will the next section be about?" that lead her to use the table of contents, the index, and chapter headings to answer.

➤ Point out graphs, charts, and other types of graphics, and talk about what they show. Have your child create charts and graphs of her own. For additional graphing activities, see Statistics and Probability, page 185.

Build a Reference Library

No matter what encyclopedia salespeople tell you, you don't have to spend a fortune to build a perfectly adequate reference library in your home. Here's how:

• Scan library sales, Salvation Army or Goodwill stores, want ads, and yard sales for discarded sets or encyclopedias, dictionaries, and other reference books. Even an old set is better than none. You might not find the answer to the question about the Berlin Wall, but Harry Houdini and the platypus ought to be in there!

• Buy a current almanac, such as *Information Please* or *World Almanac*. Paperback almanacs are often available at cut-rate prices. Check your child's school book club or large retail stores.

HAVE MORE TIME?

➤ Play Fictionary. This game requires three or more players and a dictionary.

FICTIONARY

1. One player chooses an unknown word from the dictionary.
2. Other players write a mock definition on slips of paper, using dictionary style, while the player who chose the word copies down the real definition (just one meaning).
3. The player who knows the real definition reads all of the responses.
4. All players try to guess which definition is the correct one. Players get a point for choosing the correct definition. The player who chose the word gets a point each time another player chooses a wrong definition.

➤ Use reference works to solve crossword and other word puzzles together. Using reference books isn't cheating. It's learning. What is a city in Portugal that begins with *L*? Use an encyclopedia or an atlas. What is another word for *evil*? Use a dictionary or a thesaurus. Who won the Academy Award for best actress in 1998? Check an almanac.

Organizing Information

Fourth grade is a time for report writing, and finding the information is only part of the challenge. Sometimes—at least for the parent—organizing that information seems like 99 percent of the job. Two basic strategies will help make this task easier for your child:

1. Survey the material (known in educational circles as skimming and scanning).
2. Use graphic organizers to keep track of the information.

HAVE FIVE MINUTES?

➤ Teach your child the basics of skimming and scanning. Open a nonfiction book of your child's choice and ask "What do you want to find out?" Look at chapter headings, picture captions, and graphics. Ask "Have we found the answer yet?" If so, great. If not, ask "Do you have an idea where in the book we might find the answer?"

➤ Show your child how to take notes on note cards.

1. Write only *one* note on each card.

2. Write down only those words needed to remember the information.

3. Place all the note cards on a table and sort them according to which notes belong together. Your child may want to color code or number all the cards that belong in one group. This step is very difficult for many fourth graders, but it is vitally important. If your child can master this grouping process, she is well on her way to writing a well-organized paper.

4. Now help your child decide the order in which she wants to present her information, and place the groups of cards in that order.

5. Your child might learn how to write a formal outline (with Roman numerals and letters) this year. If not, show her how to use the groups of cards to create a simple numbered outline, as shown.

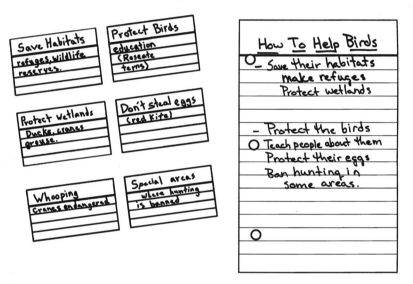

➤ Practice using key words. Suggest that your child close her eyes while you read aloud a brief article from a newspaper or magazine. Encourage her to try to form a picture in her mind of what you are reading about. After you have finished reading, ask her to give you *one word* that tells about the passage you just read.

HAVE MORE TIME?

➤ Show your child how to use a KWL chart. Use the chart in the back of the book, or fold a sheet of paper in thirds. Ask your child to label the paper with these headings: "What I *Know*," "What I *Want* to Know," "What I *Learned*" (or simply, K-W-L). Before your child does his research, ask him to record what he already knows about the subject in the first column. Then have him write what he wants to know in the second column. Tell him that it's fine to add to this column as he reads. Finally, as your child completes his research, have him record what he has learned.

➤ Encourage your child to use drawings (graphic organizers) to keep track of information. How your child "sees" information might be very different from how you do. Show her a few classic formats (see the graphic organizers on pages 213–15 in the back of the book for starters), but then allow her to set up diagrams, lists, or charts that make sense to her.

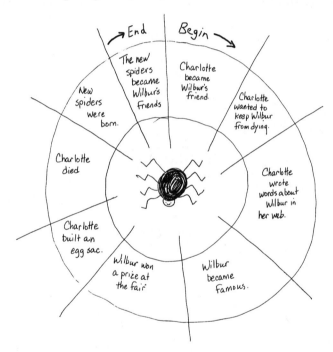

This student chose a circular graphic to represent the events in the book Charlotte's Web *by E. B. White.]*

Giving Oral Presentations

Okay. Your child has successfully collected and organized all the information she needs for her project or report. Now she has to present it. She may be asked to produce a written report. If so, you can help her by following some of the suggestions in Writing, page 105. On the other hand, fourth graders are very often asked to give oral presentations to show what they've learned. Book reports, social studies projects, and science fair entries all require skill in oral presentation. For some children, the prospect of an oral presentation is little more than a great opportunity to grab the limelight. For others, it invokes nothing short of paralyzing fear. Do all you can to help your child become comfortable with expressing herself orally. It is a skill she will need throughout her entire life.

HAVE FIVE MINUTES?

➤ Encourage the fine art of conversation. The earliest schools in America were often called Blab Schools because, due to lack of books, children learned their lessons by reciting them. Later, proper young ladies and gentlemen were given lessons in elocution and debate. Unfortunately, school days and at-home time are often so highly scheduled that there is no time for such practice in civil conversation and artful debate. Make time to talk with your child, and don't be afraid to ask challenging questions such as "So, what's the point here?" or "Why do you think that?" Like reading, writing, and learning the multiplication tables, speaking well takes practice. Here are a few suggestions of giving your child the practice she needs:

- Establish the habit of giving short recitations. Expect each family member—even the youngest—to recite one memorized passage. The passage can be a short poem, a paragraph from a novel, a section of an oral report in progress, an original piece of writing, or even, for the wee ones in the family, "Fire fire fire, raging all about. Here come the fire trucks to put the fire out!"
- Encourage open debate. Fourth graders are very serious about the issues that matter to them. Whether your child wants to change the seating patterns in the cafeteria, propose an increase in her allowance, or save the whales, your gentle questions can go a long way in showing her that a little forethought and organization can strengthen an argument significantly.
- Tell stories. Storytelling is perfect practice for public speaking. A properly told story demands that its teller keep the main idea of the story in mind, organize the story's sequence and details, and look for ways to keep the audience engaged. Fables, myths, folktales, and fairy tales all make excellent storytelling fare.

➤ Use the suggestions in the "Organizing Information" section, above, to help your child get her thoughts in order. Ask your child's teacher if she may use note cards to keep on track during the presentation.

➤ Remind your child that even the president practices the State of the Union address many times before presenting it to the American public. Encourage your child to practice her presentation in front of noncritical family members, the mirror, or even a row of stuffed animals.

HAVE MORE TIME?

➤ Encourage your child to use props. Not every child has a way with words. If your child has a way with crafts, or music, or theatrics, or charts and graphs, ask her teacher if there is a way she can use her talents as a part of her oral presentation. Most teachers (and classmates) are more than willing to have a break from the standard book or social studies report form. Here are some possibilities:
  • a play or skit
  • a puppet show
  • a comic strip or collection of illustrations
  • a time line or calendar
  • a handbill or advertisement
  • a ballad, jingle, or rap lyrics
  • a board game
  • a model or map
  • a monologue or dialogue between two characters
  • a letter or diary

Struggling Readers

Children who are below grade level in reading are often referred to by educators as "reluctant readers." By fourth grade, children who have not begun to read with considerable fluency might appear to be reluctant. They probably groan when assigned reading skill work or research that requires reading. They likely avoid reading aloud or answering comprehension questions in class. No doubt they choose the thinnest books with the fewest number of words per page—and, yes, they even fake reading.

But reluctant? Hardly. No one would choose the plight of the poor performing reader. Struggling to decode words, to make sense of multisyllabic words, to create meaning from print is hard and often embarrassing work. No, the term "struggling reader" better defines these children.

Fourth graders who are stumbling, reading word by painful word, desperately need your assistance. First of all, they need you to be their advocate. If your child has not been identified as one who needs additional reading support and/or special school services, talk to his teacher. Suggest that your child be tested for any problems, such as learning disability, that might be getting in the way of his reading.

Second, you must create a safe and supportive reading environment at home. Poor readers do not need more time with flashcards or completing skill workbooks. They need two things: one-to-one support and lots of time spent actually reading. You are in the best position to provide both of these requirements. Tell your child that you will help him to grow into a capable and confident reader. Here are some ways to begin.

- Establish a time when you and your child can read together each day. Do not use this time as punishment by saying things like "Until you get your grades up, we're going to sit here and read." You also shouldn't take it away as reward: "If you clean your room today, you can skip reading time." Practice reading in the same nurturing and supportive way that you might help your child learn to make a grilled cheese sandwich or catch a baseball. Approach each session in a positive, you-can-do-it way.

- Take turns reading a book aloud. When it is your fourth grader's turn, try not to make him feel as if he's being tested. If he stumbles over a word, you might say, "I often stumble over words like that, too." If he comes to a word he doesn't know, you can ask, "What would make sense here?" or "What letter sounds do you recognize?" and then encourage him to keep going. Simply provide some words now and then to help your child keep momentum.

- Find books your child can read successfully *and* that meet his interests. Help him find stories about kids he can relate to. Your librarian will be your best resource. Remember that home is the place your child can practice reading without comparing page length, print size, or oral fluency with classmates. Don't let him label books as "baby books." Encourage him to read anything that catches his fancy and will help him feel successful.

- Until your child is reading beginning chapter books, sit down with more than one book at a time. If your child experiences success with one book, he'll probably want to start another immediately. Don't lose this perfect opportunity.

- Make reading a social event in your home. If you pressure your child to read, but everyone else is watching TV, talking on the telephone, or playing games, he'll feel isolated. Read with and beside your child. Share interesting facts or fun lines. Smile when you get to the good parts.

- Talk to your child. Let him know that you recognize his struggle and his efforts and that you have begun to search for ways to help him. By acknowledging and accepting his difficulties, you might prevent him from "faking it" as a reader. Let him know that many famous people such as Leonardo da Vinci, Thomas Edison, and Albert Einstein had reading problems. (And if that doesn't make an impression, how about Tom Cruise, Magic Johnson, or Whoopi Goldberg?)

- Children in the fourth grade often find themselves reading more than one book at a time. They may read one book during formal reading time, another during independent reading time, and yet another at home. This can be defeating for the struggling reader who is just learning to follow a story or stay involved in chapter books. If this is the case, ask your child's teacher if your child can stick with one book until completion. Suggest that he carry the book back and forth from school.
- Watch a movie with your child and then suggest he read the same story in book form. The movie will provide him with knowledge of the setting, characters and plot—a tremendous boost for the struggling reader.

Consider hiring a well-trained reading tutor. The right person or program can often launch the struggling reader.

For support and ideas, see some of the books listed below. Your library might have many more resources not listed here.

- *Solving Your Child's Reading Problems,* by Ricki Linksman (Citadel Press)
- *Unicorns are Real,* by Barbara Meister Vitale (Warner)
- *Unlocking Your Child's Learning Potential,* by Cheri Fuller (Pinon)
- *Keys to Parenting a Child with a Learning Disability,* by Barry E. McNamara and Francine J. McNamara (Barrons)
- *Parenting a Child with a Learning Disability: A Practical, Empathetic Guide,* by Cheryl Gerson Tuttle and Penny Paquette (Lowell House)
- *Taming the Dragons: Real Help for School Problems,* by Susan Setley (Starfish)

Writing Exercises

The checklist in the Writing Assessment, along with the student survey in the For Kids Only booklet, will help you to know which Writing Activities are most appropriate for your child.

Most fourth graders write a lot. They record the events of their lives in daily journals. They note their reactions to literature in book reports and literary journals. They write social studies reports and science logs. Even in math they document their procedures for solving a problem.

You might have noticed that your fourth grader's writing is vastly improved from last year. Her sentences are more complete and coherent than they were a year ago. Her spelling, though certainly not perfect, generally follows standard rules. Even her handwriting is likely to have improved. By all accounts, fourth grade writers should be in their prime.

Unfortunately, many fourth graders don't see things that way. Students who just a year ago were writing fantastic stories with elaborate plots can suddenly seem paralyzed. Their stories are stilted and formulaic. The prospect of writing a page-long report brings desperate tears. Why? What might cause a child's willingness to write to falter just when she finally has so many tools at her fingertips?

In fact, those very writing skills that should be a fourth grader's strength might actually be working against her creativity. She is much more aware of the "right" way to do things than she was even a year ago. She is highly conscious of her own errors and may be hesitant to take the risks that are the hallmark of good writing. In order to get over this writing hump, your child is going to need your help. Here's how.

Provide lots of time and opportunities to write. Familiarity breeds comfort. Take any opportunity you can to show your child the usefulness and fun of writing. Talk about your own writing—the peer evaluation you sweated over for a coworker, the silly E-mail you sent along to Uncle George. Make sure you have lots of writing tools available—fun stationery, neon pens, Post-it notes, sharpened pencils, and plenty of erasers. Remember, fourth graders love *stuff*. Keep in mind that writing does not have to be a solitary endeavor. In fact, your fourth grader may do her best writing at the kitchen table with you available to respond to her occasional "So how does this sound?"

Respect and appreciate your child's writing. Suppose your child asks you to read her impassioned letter to the U.S. Fish and Wildlife Service on the subject of hunting endangered woodland caribou. How do you respond?

- "You misspelled *caribou*."
- "I'm not really sure people in federal agencies read letters from kids."
- "You know, hunting is one way of keeping wildlife populations under control. I don't think you really understand this issue."

Remember that no matter how you might feel about the grammar or spelling or even the content of your child's writing, that writing is *your child's*. Although it might be possible to gently guide a bit of revision (see Revising, page 110), do everything in your power not to undermine your child's pride of ownership. Writing can be slow, tiresome, scary work. Give your child's writing the same respect you would give your child herself. Simply saying "You've really thought about this, haven't you? Do you see any changes you'd like to make before you send your letter off?" might be the most appropriate response.

Take the process of learning to write seriously. Reading and math both have their processes. You assume that your child will learn how to approach a math problem or a page of text systematically. Yet, too often, when it comes to writing, children are left to fend for themselves with little more than a few workbook pages on nouns and verbs to guide them. No wonder many children seem to have the notion that there is something magical about writing well! There are natural steps that make up the process of writing just as there are natural steps that make up the process of solving a math problem.

These steps are:

- Prewriting, when the writer decides why she's writing (her purpose), what she wants to say, and what form she wants to put her writing in.
- Writing, when the writer gets the words down on paper.
- Revising, when the writer adds, subtracts, and rearranges the *content* to make her writing clearer.

- Editing, when the writer proofreads for grammar, spelling, and punctuation errors.

The entire process might seem overwhelming—certainly it is to the average fourth grader. Remember, your goal is to *keep your child writing*. Break writing up into little bits, never expect perfection, and above all, keep the writing you do at home as pressure-free as possible.

Prewriting

HAVE FIVE MINUTES?

➤ Introduce your child to a wide variety of writing formats. You can do this by bringing home books that contain letters, personal narratives, descriptions, articles, or nonfiction reports. Ask your librarian to show you books with different formats, or look for some of the books listed here. By exposing your child to as many formats as possible, you will help her to make more creative choices when choosing her own format, and you will give her wonderful models to emulate.

➤ Encourage your child to keep a journal. Give her a special notebook or diary, or just suggest that she write bits about each day on a special calendar. The habit of journal writing can last throughout your child's entire life if it is given a gentle nudge now.

➤ Keep a family quotation book. Have you ever been on the telephone with your child's grandparent and said, "Oh! Junior said the most amazing thing the other day—now what was it?" Place a spiral notebook and a pen in a convenient spot, and when those amazing words come out of that amazing mouth, record them. Later, when your child is looking for something to write about, flip through the quotation book. Something in there might spark an idea.

➤ Make music part of your daily life. Sing, dance, and play the piano (or the kazoo). All these activities engage children in the rhythm and rhyme that are the basis of poetry. And don't be surprised if your child begins to make up a few extra verses of her own!

HAVE MORE TIME?

➤ Encourage your child to use a story map or other graphic organizer (see pages 215–17) to brainstorm ideas for her writing.

BOOKS THAT MODEL DIFFERENT WRITING FORMATS

Personal narratives:
- *What Do Fish Have to Do with Anything?*, by Avi (Candlewick)
- *Amelia's Notebook,* by Marissa Moss (Tricycle Press)
- *Author: A True Story,* by Helen Lester (Houghton Mifflin)
- *My Name Is Seepeetza,* by Shirley Sterling (Groundwood)

Descriptions:
- *Hawk, I'm Your Brother,* by Byrd Baylor (Scribner's)
- *Eye of the Storm: Chasing Storms with Warren Faidley,* by Warren Faidley (Putnam)
- *While a Tree Was Growing,* by Jane Bosveld (Workman)

Letters:
- *Dear Levi: Letters from the Overland Trail,* by Elvira Woodruff (Knopf)
- *Dear Mr. Henshaw,* by Beverly Cleary (Avon)
- *Love Letters,* by Arnold Adoff (Scholastic)

Reports:
- *The Egyptian News,* by Scott Steedman (Candlewick)
- *Volcano: The Eruption and Healing of Mount St. Helens,* by Patricia Lauber (Bradbury)
- *The Wright Brothers: How They Invented the Airplane,* by Russell Freedman (Holiday House)

Stories:
- *The Girl Who Dreamed Only Geese and Other Tales of the Far North,* by Howard Norman (Harcourt)
- *The Cow-Tail Switch and Other West African Stories,* by Harold Courlander and George Herzog (Holt)
- *The Dark-Thirty: Southern Tales of the Supernatural,* by Patricia McKissack (Knopf)

Poems:
- *Everywhere Faces Everywhere,* by James Berry (Simon and Schuster)
- *The Random House Book of Poetry for Children,* edited by Jack Prelutsky (Random House)
- *Sad Underwear and other Complications,* by Judith Viorst (Atheneum)

➤Encourage your fourth grader to tell stories: "And then—and then—and then—" These words are the seeds of a story, or a letter, or a report. Telling stories invites immediate feedback. When your child goes to write the story down, chances are she'll keep the section that provoked welcome laughter and she'll cut the section where she began to lose her audience.

➤ Suggest that your child draw a picture, make a sculpture out of Play-Doh, or act out her story before writing. Sometimes nonverbal means of communication can help extend and clarify ideas.

➤ Use the five-finger method for brainstorming events.

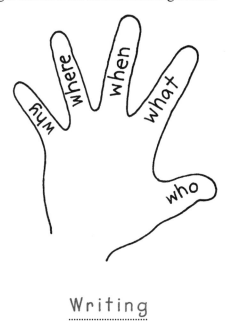

Writing

HAVE FIVE MINUTES?

➤ Give your child reasons to write in a variety of formats. In school, most fourth graders learn how to write personal narratives, descriptions, informal (and sometimes formal) letters, reports, stories, and poems. The more informal opportunities your child has to write in each of these formats at home, the easier writing will become.
  • Personal narratives: What is the best thing that has happened in your life? How did the Christmas pageant go this year? How did you solve that problem with that bully at school?
  • Descriptions: Your new house, your old dog, the best present you can imagine ever receiving.
  • Letters: Thank-you notes, fan letters, pen-pal letters, letters to the editor or the president, postcards. And don't forget E-mail!
  • Reports: On school lunches, on an endangered animal, on the exploration of Mars, on how to be a good little brother (written by a big sister, of course).

- Stories: Rewritten fairy tales, sequels to books, how the __ got its __ stories (*pourquoi* stories), tall tales, dreams.
- Poems: Limericks, senses poems, tongue twisters, nonsense poems, jingles, haiku.

Tell your child, "Just get the words on the paper." Don't worry about organization, form, or spelling at this point. Just encourage your child to write.

➤ Set up a family bulletin board or mount a memo board on the refrigerator. Encourage your child to use the board to make announcements.

➤ Post-its, or sticky notes, come in a variety of shapes and colors. Give your child a package of sticky notes to use however he wishes: a reminder to wear his uniform on Tuesday stuck on his mirror, a silly rhyme stuck on his sister's bedroom door, an "I Love You" note attached to Mom or Dad's pillow or briefcase.

HAVE MORE TIME?

➤ Encourage spontaneous writing. Did you break your brother's virtual pet? Write an apology. Did your cat eat your goldfish? Write a classified ad. Is there a great offer for trading cards on the back of the cereal box? Send off for them now. Use any opportunity that pops up during the day to show your child the value of writing.

➤ Help your child create a family or neighborhood newsletter. As chief reporter, he might gather news, conduct interviews, give a calendar of events, and include a page of funny jokes or quotations.

➤ Reread *Harriet the Spy*, give your child a notebook, and encourage him to spy.

➤ If you don't think you can stand listening to one more play-by-play rehash of a baseball game or Disney movie, have your child write it down. You might want to read a short newspaper article or review to serve as a model for your young reporter.

➤ Give your child responsibility for his own "business" writing. If he needs a note for school, have him write it (you'll still have to sign it). If he's packing for camp, have him write his own packing list. If he's got soccer practice on Tuesday, make sure that he's the one who writes it on the family calendar.

Revising

Many people think of revising and editing as two names for the same part of the writing process; that is, the postwriting part, when everything is tidied up. In fact, revising and editing are very different processes. During the revision stage, a writer makes changes in the *content* of a piece of writing: Have I said what I meant to say? Do the ideas make sense, or are they all jumbled up? Is there information missing, or have I added details that don't seem related?

Most fourth graders know how to proofread a first draft in preparation for writing a final draft, and they assume that revising is the same as proofreading. By fourth grade, children are ready to add an intermediary step between writing and proofreading—that of looking critically at their own content, the meaning of their writing. Unfortunately, getting words onto paper is hard work, and many fourth graders (and adults) are loath to change what they have already written. Showing your child that getting the words onto paper is just a first step—that there will be time to rethink, reorganize, and rewrite if necessary—can actually lighten the task of the "ideas into words" step. It can be a great relief for the hypercritical fourth grader to realize that a writer's work does not always have to be perfect.

HAVE FIVE MINUTES?

➤ Show your child one of your own first drafts. Let your child see that "real" writers rarely "get it right" on the first try. Keep the first draft of something you have written recently—a report you have written for work or a letter to the landlord, perhaps—and compare it to the final draft. What did you change? Why?

➤ Suggest that your child read one paragraph aloud at a time. Ask, "Do all these sentences tell about the same thing? Which ones don't seem to be related? Are there any other details you want to add to this paragraph?"

➤ Talk about sequencing. Discuss which order makes the most sense for the writing at hand.

Support or Criticism?

Be extremely sensitive about how you react to your fourth grader's writing. Remember, fourth graders are not known for their tolerance of criticism! It might help to keep these two ground rules in mind:

1. Make sure that your first and strongest reaction is positive. A fourth grader can see right through "Uh-huh, this is nice, but what about . . . ?" Look for what is good about your child's writing, talk about it first, and be specific.

2. Question, don't criticize. Choose one aspect of your child's writing to comment on and phrase it as a question. "Can a person who doesn't know the story figure out what happened when?" is a lot easier on your young writer's ears than "You've got the events in the wrong order here!"

➤If possible, encourage your child to work on a computer. Word processing programs make it easy for your child to rearrange, add, and delete words and paragraphs and take a lot of the drudgery out of the revision process. If you don't have access to a computer, cut the sentences apart and try rearranging them in a different order.

HAVE MORE TIME?

➤Help your child create a revision checklist to guide her in revising her own work when you are not around.

> ☐ Does my story or report have a clear beginning, middle, and end?
>
> ☐ Do I need to add any information?
>
> ☐ Is the information in an order that makes sense?

➤Show your child how to use a diagram to organize her thoughts. Until young writers become adept at structuring their own writing, it is sometimes helpful to give them a structure to follow.

For stories:

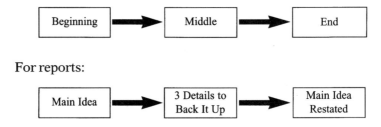

For reports:

For more suggestions about organization, see Study Skills, page 91.

Editing

Not every piece of writing your child does will—or should—go through the editing process. Writers need many opportunities to experiment and record their thoughts freely. By fourth grade, however, most children are expected to turn in formal assignments that demonstrate standard conventions of grammar and spelling. Since few writers can concentrate on content and writing conventions at the same time, it stands to reason that most of the writing that your child will do in school will go through some kind of editing process.

If your child asks for help in the editing process, be sure to remember the cardinal rule: *Respond to content first.* Only after you have remarked positively and enthusiastically about your child's ideas is it appropriate to help tidy up his writing.

Most fourth grade teachers expect their students to be able to edit for:

- grammar, punctuation, and capitalization
- spelling
- handwriting

Grammar, Capitalization, and Punctuation

In fourth grade, your child will continue to fine-tune his understanding of the way sentences are put together and the correct ways to use words. Some fourth grade teachers use grammar textbooks and worksheets to accomplish this task. Others teach these skills by responding to the children's individual writing. If you think of grammar and mechanics as the nuts and bolts of writing, it makes sense that, like nuts and bolts, they need to be connected to something in order to fulfill their function. Young children who are taught grammar and mechanics as isolated skills are often unable to apply those skills when it comes time to write.

What does this mean for you as a parent? Yes, your child needs to learn grammar. His effectiveness in both spoken and written language count on it. But you can best help your child gain an ease and understanding of language by *using it*—by reading and writing and playing with the English language. Any of the activities in the Reading Exercises and Writing Exercises chapters of this book will help further this aim. In addition, you might try a few of these:

> Suggest that your child remember the word *chips* when editing her work.
>
> C —Did I use capital letters where they are needed?
>
> H —Is my handwriting legible?
>
> I —Did I indent at the beginning of each paragraph?
>
> P —Did I use punctuation correctly?
>
> S —Did I spell all the words correctly?

HAVE FIVE MINUTES?

➤ As you respond to your child's writing, use the language of grammar. *"Vanquished!* Wow, what a great adjective!" or "What are some other verbs you could use for *said*?"

➤ As you go about your Saturday errands, grow a sentence. Start with a simple declarative sentence, such as "The bee buzzed." Then take turns adding a word or phrase to expand the sentence as much as possible. ("The big bee buzzed." "The big bee buzzed in my ear.")

➤ Make up Hink Pinks. Hink Pinks (or Hinky Pinkies or Hinkety Pinketies, depending on the number of syllables used) consist of an adjective and a noun that rhyme. Trade clues back and forth and see who gets stumped first. Here are a few to get you started.
- A thin bird (a narrow sparrow).
- A happier dog (a merrier terrier).
- A tall animal's giggle (a giraffe's laugh).

➤ Make up Tom Swifties. Devising Tom Swifties is a humorous way to practice using adverbs. Once your child gets the hang of it, he will love making up his own. Here are a couple of classics:
- "This lemonade needs more sugar," Tom said *sourly*.
- "I adore seafood," Tom said *crabbily*.
- "Give me that knife," Tom said *sharply*.

➤ Have your child go through a newspaper article with a bright pen and highlight the quotation marks she finds. Point out paragraph indentation.

➤ If your child doesn't already know how to address an envelope, now's the time to teach him. Addresses afford great opportunities for discussing capitalization and punctuation conventions.

HAVE MORE TIME?

➤ Suggest that your child create his own Mad Libs. Most fourth graders are familiar with the format of Mad Libs, where they fill in blanks with nouns, verbs, adjectives, and adverbs to create silly stories.

➤ Go on a sentence fragment hunt. Tell your child that a fragment is a sentence without a subject (who or what) or a verb (action word). "That dog!" is a sentence fragment. So is "Running in circles again." Invite him to search through a newspaper or magazine and circle any sentence fragments he can find. Then work together to turn each one into a complete sentence.

➤ Magnetic Poetry for Kids is a commercially produced collection of magnetized words. Place a set of words on the refrigerator or a cookie sheet for family members to create silly sentences. Then talk about the sentences. Are they grammatically correct? Why or why not?

If you wish to make your own set of magnetic words, look for magnetic sheets wherever office supplies are sold. Snip the sheets into word-size strips. Use an indelible marker to write words of your choice on the strips.

➤ Copy a short, fairly easy paragraph from one of your child's books or magazines, but do not include any capitalization or punctuation. Invite your child to read the paragraph. Does he run into trouble? Next, give him a bright marker and have him add the necessary punctuation. Whew! That's better!

Spelling

Your fourth grader has come a long way since those first and second grade days when it was hard to decipher exactly what "the ct csd the dg" actually meant. Chances are, most of the words in your child's written work are now properly spelled, or are at least close approximations. Still, the English language continues to confound. At times there seem to be more exceptions than rules, and even children who are fairly comfortable with language can grow pretty frustrated. To make matters worse, by fourth grade, children—if not their parents and teachers as well—have often separated themselves into "good spellers" and "bad spellers." If you run into an adult who blithely confesses, "I always was a terrible speller," most likely that attitude took hold somewhere around the fourth grade.

Weekly spelling lists are routine in many fourth grades, though their sources vary. Some lists might contain words from a spelling textbook, others from a book the class is reading or a particular area of study. How your child goes about studying these lists depends in part on the words themselves (do the words follow a spelling pattern?) and in part on your child's schedule. See the recommendations for studying spelling lists below.

You might never know why your child has a particularly easy or difficult time with spelling. (Theorists have been going at this one for years.) Bad spellers are legendary—Albert Einstein, Thomas Edison, and George Washington among them. What you *can* do is give your child as many tools as possible,

Help your child establish a system for studying her weekly spelling list. Here is one standard approach:

1. Your child writes each word on an index card.
2. She sorts the cards in any way that makes sense. Are there any similarities among the words? Do many of them start with *th* or have a silent *e* in them?
3. Give your child a pretest. Say each word and have her spell it aloud or write it down. Put any words she knows in a separate pile.
4. Your child studies the remaining words. Talk about each word. For example, "What do you already know about this word? How many syllables does this word have?" Then your child says each word aloud and writes it on a sheet of paper.

Test again. Put aside any words she now knows and repeat step 4 with the others.

including a basic knowledge of spelling patterns and mnemonic devices (*and* computer spell-checkers *and* a good dictionary), so that spelling doesn't get in the way of his ability to write.

HAVE FIVE MINUTES?

➤ Encourage your child to read. The more your child reads, the more visual images of words she will form in her mind. Even if your child doesn't know how to spell *necessary,* if she has seen the word enough times, she might at least know that *necessery* doesn't look right and can turn to the dictionary.

➤ Play Ghost. There are two ways to play this classic game. Here are the rules to the make-a-word version.

GHOST

1. The first player starts with a letter that is also a word, such as *I.*
2. The second player adds a letter to make a new word, such as *in.*
3. The next player adds another letter to make another word, such as *tin* or *nip.*
4. The player who cannot make a new word gets the letter *G.* The first player to receive *G–H–O–S–T* loses.
5. The don't-make-a-word version is played similarly, except that players try *not* to make a word. However, they must have a word in mind as they add letters. For example, the second player might add *i* to *e* to make *ie,* as long as he can give the word *lie* or *believe* if challenged by another player.

➤ Look for consistent troublemakers in your child's writing. Suggest that your child write her spelling demons on Post-it notes and stick them on her desk or inside her writing notebook.

➤ Exaggerate the pronunciation of difficult words to emphasize the spelling pattern, for example, "pe-o-ple."

➤ Suggest that your child use her spelling words to make a crossword puzzle.

➤ Challenge each other with spelling riddles, such as "It looks like it should rhyme with *beard* but it doesn't" (*heard*).

➤ Use the words to play Hangman.

➤ Play Scrabble, Anagrams, or Boggle. All are excellent games for practicing spelling.

➤ If your child's spelling demons seem to follow a pattern, such as vowels with *r* (Is it *humer* or *humor*?), help her brainstorm a list of words that follow the same spelling pattern. Encourage her to keep the list in her writing notebook or in a personal dictionary.

If your child is bringing home spelling lists and standard study methods don't seem to be working, your child may need to go about it in a different way. Not everybody learns in the same way. Some people need to see something before they can commit it to memory. Others need to hear it. Still others need to *do* it. You might already have a pretty good idea of how your child learns best. If not, help your child to pick and choose from the following list—one strategy a week—until she finds one that works for her.

Visual Strategies
- Write the word in one color. Then close your eyes and visualize the word in that color. (The color need not relate to the word; some people simply retain images in their minds with the help of color.)
- Write each letter of the word in a different color.
- Find the word in magazines, newspapers, or junk mail. Circle it or cut it out.
- Write the word in large letters on an index card. Cut around the word so that you can see the shape of the word.

Fourth Grade Spelling Demons

There are some spelling demons that many fourth graders still need extra help with include:

- **Homophones:** *to/two/too, their/there, knew/new, whether/weather* (see also page 87)
- **Words with apostrophes:** contractions (*it's, they're*) and possessives (*puppy's, puppies'*)
- **Vowels with *r*:** *worn, firm, earn, burn, favorite, proper*
- **Final *l* sound:** *handle, nickel, total, metal*
- **Letter combinations -*eigh*, -*ough*, and -*augh*:** *weight, freight, though, enough, caught*
- **Soft *g* or *c* sound:** *manage, dodge, cage, chance, fragrance*

Kinesthetic or Tactile Strategies
- Write the word in shaving cream, salt on a cookie sheet, sand, or mud.
- Write the word in huge letters in the air.
- Use magnetic letters, Scrabble tiles, or letter cards to spell the word.
- Use a flashlight to spell the word on a darkened wall.
- Have someone trace the letters of a word on your back. Guess what the word is. Then switch roles.
- Draw the word in giant letters on the pavement (or use masking tape on the floor). Walk, skip, or hop along the letters.
- Type the word on a typewriter or computer keyboard.

Auditory Strategies
- As you write the word, whisper or shout each letter.
- Sing the word to a familiar tune:
  K-n-i-f-e, k-n-i-f-e
  Heigh-ho the knife-io, k-n-i-f-e.

Handwriting

"Does it have to be in cursive?" In most fourth grade classrooms, this plaintive question is a common one. By fourth grade, most children have learned how to form both printed and cursive letters. In a typical fourth grade, however, the handwriting on papers mounted on bulletin boards still ranges from careful, every-letter-perfectly-formed (with *i*'s dotted with circles or even smiley faces) masterpieces to the painful struggles of those who obviously are just trying to get the words on the paper.

Whether handwriting is emphasized in your child's classroom depends upon your child's teacher, the school's curriculum, and the current fashion in educational circles. Still, sad but true, throughout your child's academic career, her writing—her ability to express her ideas on paper—will be inextricably linked to her handwriting ability. The child who finds the physical task of writing agonizing most likely will simply not like to write. The teacher who struggles to read a barely legible composition most likely will not make the time or effort to appreciate the fine ideas that lie behind the scrawl. Many fourth graders still struggle with handwriting. What can a parent do to help?

First, talk with your child's teacher about his or her expectations. Must all children use the cursive writing system currently taught in your child's school, or are children allowed to use whatever style is easiest and most legible for them—even if it is a combination of styles (which is the case for most adults)? How you can help with handwriting will depend greatly upon the expectations placed on your individual child. Above all, remember, *never* place a child's handwriting skills above her written expression—that is, her chance to say what she wants to say in writing. If your child has a story to tell, let her tell it however she can. Don't let anything—even handwriting—stand in the way.

HAVE FIVE MINUTES?

➤ If your child must use a certain style, make sure you know which style it is (D'Nealian and Zaner Bloser are two of the most common). Then ask your child's teacher to give you a copy of the letter forms. Make more copies and place them wherever your child might need them—on her desk, in the front of her writing notebook, even taped into the inside of her backpack. Many children just can't remember "how to make a—." Having a reference handy will help.

➤ Look carefully at your child's writing. Do the lines of writing slant up or down, or even off the paper? Do the words run together? Help your child make a guide for her writing—perhaps a sheet of paper with lines and margins heavily marked in black to place beneath her "final copy" sheet. Or perhaps she might place a paper clip or other slender object between words to help her keep track of word spacing. These guides often serve as security blankets for children who have just too much to think about as they write.

➤ Make sure your child's paper is properly positioned. Do not assume that how a child places her paper is how she wants it. Good paper placement can even relieve a left-handed writer of the awkward "left-hand hook." Work with your child to figure out what position gives her the straightest, most legible, and comfortable way to write.

➤ Finally, take heart that technology is available to help your child become a legible writer. If your child truly hates forming letters by hand, do all you can to get her access to a word-processing program on a computer. Even if she takes twice as long to pick out each letter on the keyboard as she might have writing the words by hand, the resulting legibility might free her writing in ways you never imagined. Many schools begin keyboarding classes in the fourth grade. If you have a home computer, you might encourage your child to try one of these software programs to increase her keyboarding speed:
  • UltraKey, by Bytes of Learning
  • Type to Learn, by Sunburst Communications
  • Mavis Beacon Teaches Typing for Kids, by Mindscape

Reading and Writing Enrichment

So you've got yourself an avid reader, a nose-in-a-book, can't-put-it-down, flashlight-under-the-covers gem of a reader. Or perhaps you've got yourself a passionate writer, one who writes outrageously funny satires of family holiday get-togethers or spends hours on the front stoop writing verse after verse. Or perhaps you've got yourself a kid who likes to read and likes to write and is looking for a little more direction from you. If you've read the other parts of this book, you know that fourth grade is a slippery time for even the best readers and writers. Other distractions, such as friends and outside activities, quietly threaten to pull your child away from the reading and writing that have given him so much pleasure in the past. To support your avid reader or writer, you must find a way to keep him challenged, to keep him involved with other children (a fourth grade priority for even the most individualistic child), and to keep him aware of your love of his loves—reading and writing.

HAVE FIVE MINUTES?

➤ Keep reading with your child. Read aloud to him. Listen as he reads to you. If all else fails, get an extra copy of the book and read it on your own. Do not assume that, just because he can read anything, your child understands everything. More than ever, this child needs your involvement. If you encourage him to choose his own reading material (which you should), he is bound to run across concepts and emotional issues that are simply over his head. To learn how to evaluate and expand upon what he has read, your child needs someone to talk to about his reading. That person is you.

➤ Can't-fill-'em-up readers can be hard to satisfy, and no matter how delightful the challenge is, finding books to suggest for your avid reader can be a trial. Together, explore the different genres in *But That's Another Story,* edited by Sandy Asher (Walker). This book contains stories that represent each of the genres along with a description of the genre and an author interview. If your child takes a liking to a certain author or genre, you can follow up with a trip to the library.

➤ Delve deeper into words and their origins:
  • Clipped words: words that have been shortened, such as *sub* for *submarine* or *movie* for *moving picture*
  • "Portmanteau" words: words that have two meanings combined into one word, such as *brunch* (breakfast + lunch) and *squiggle* (squirm + wiggle)
  • Words borrowed from names, such as teddy bear (after Teddy Roosevelt) or hamburger (after Hamburg, Germany)
  • Acronyms, such as VIP or RSVP

➤ Search headlines for puns and other forms of word play.

➤ Talk about the methods that advertisements and commercials use to persuade people to buy their products.

HAVE MORE TIME?

➤ Find out when authors are appearing at local bookstores for book signings and readings, and take your child.

➤ Encourage your child to become the family historian. Suggest that he interview family members, record information about family heirlooms, and start a collection of old family yarns or recipes.

➤ Suggest a reading sleepover. Encourage each guest invited to the party to bring a favorite book. After the guests share bits of their books, give special prizes for the funniest, weirdest, scariest, or saddest passages. Or play Charades by pantomiming book titles and famous characters. For snacks, prepare foods from some of your child's favorite books.

➤ Invite your child to make a time line of his life. String a piece of sturdy clothesline across one wall of his room and help him use masking tape to divide the line into years. Get out your child's baby book, school records, or photos and suggest that he choose items to clip to the line in the proper order. As he continues to add current paraphernalia, you might have to extend the line to the other walls as well.

➤ Encourage your child to preserve his writing by making a book. By this time, your child probably knows how to make simple books by stapling pages together with a construction paper cover. For variety, you might suggest alternative methods such as these.

PAGES
- Cut pages into different shapes. Is it a book about soccer? Make it in the shape of a soccer ball.
- Punch holes in index cards and hold them together with metal rings.
- A home computer is a great self-publishing tool. Many word-processing programs include page templates that will allow your child to move her writing about the page and insert clip-art illustrations.

COVERS
- Have your child illustrate sheets of poster board. Protect the illustrated covers with clear Con-Tact paper.
- Use a report folder or looseleaf binder as a cover. Your child will be able to add, subtract, or rearrange his book pages whenever he pleases.

BINDING
- Clear plastic covers are perfect for giving stapled books a more permanent feel. The plastic strips slide over the staples, and the clear plastic protects the page within.
- Punch holes in the pages and hold them together with yarn, string, ribbon, metal rings, or leather ties—even plastic bag twisties will do in a pinch!
- For a special treat, take your child's masterpiece to a copy shop and have it spiral- or comb-bound.

READY-MADE BOOKS
- Watch sales tables for items that would make good books. Small spiral-bound notebooks, blank journals, and travel diaries are all good substitutes for a hand-made book.
- Slip the pages of your child's book between the plastic sheets of a photo album.

- Make-your-own-book kits of various sorts are available in toy catalogs and book and toy stores. One such kit, by Chimeric, provides
book pages that your child can complete and send back to the manu-
facturer to have bound into a book.

Math Exercises

Problem Solving

The ability to approach problems in a variety of ways is measured by questions 2, 3, 7, 9, and 14 on the Math Assessment.

"I've never been good in math."

"Math has never been my thing."

"I've always hated math!"

Do these phrases sound familiar? Perhaps you have said something along these lines yourself. Yet, try replacing the word *math* with, say, *reading*. It's hard to imagine someone at a cocktail party glibly announcing, "Reading has never been my thing!" While few people question the pleasure of sitting down with a good book, many are hard-pressed to find the comfort or joy of getting their hands on a good math problem.

Math anxiety, fear of math, drill and kill—no matter what they're called, negative attitudes toward math prevail. At the same time, nearly all parents—even those who say "I've always hated math"—are deeply concerned about their own children's competence in mathematics. They know that their children will need math skills to function in everyday life, to buy groceries, to pay taxes, even to communicate in this ever more technological world. They also sense from their own experiences that a person who is anxious about math is at a definite disadvantage in this world. On the other hand, the person who approaches numbers comfortably and playfully seems to have the world at her fingertips.

Every parent would like his or her child to have the world at her fingertips. But just now you might have a fourth grader in front of you who has not the world but a sheet of twenty-five long division problems at her fingertips. And she's crying.

Although you probably can't convince your child (or anyone!) that a sheet of division problems is fun, you *can* do everything in your power to create an environment in which your child's confidence in solving problems can flourish. How? By doing what you did long before long division, by challenging your child to solve her own problems ("You can put on your own socks!" you said to your toddler so many years ago), by celebrating successes ("That's right! You need *two* socks!"), and by downplaying mistakes ("You almost got it! Let's turn this one around"). The problem-solving skills your child needed to dress herself as a toddler are at heart the same skills she will need to approach the mathematical problems of her future. By nourishing those skills at home, you can help your child build the confidence that will take the misery out of math. Here's how.

1. Find the fun in mathematics.
2. Model persistence and spunk.
3. Share problem-solving strategies.

Finding the Fun in Mathematics

HAVE FIVE MINUTES?

➤ Use the fun that your child is already having. What does your child love? Soccer? Gymnastics? Computer games? Virtual pets? No matter what your child's passion is, math probably has more to do with it than either of you realize. Can your baseball fan rattle off every one of her favorite players' averages? Ask her how she might go about finding her own average. Does your animal lover want to make a maze for her pet rat? Discuss strategies for designing it. Just remember, *the passion comes first*. "Let's think about different ways we can organize your horse collection" is a far cry from "Okay, now divide your horses into six groups. How many in each group?" Your job is to highlight the math, not direct it. Too much direction will kill both the passion and the math.

➤ As you wait anywhere, anytime, challenge each other to find the math in the jobs you see going on around you. Although it's easier to find the math in some jobs (bank teller) than others (firefighter), it probably won't take long to realize that all occupations use math in one way or another.

Besides being fun, this activity heads off the inevitable whine, "But when am I ever gonna use this?"

➤ Tempt each other with math riddles. You think you're so smart? Share one of these with your child and see who comes up with the answer first.

1. Two U.S. coins total fifty-five cents. One is not a nickel. What are the coins? (HINT: the answer is in the sentence "One is not a nickel.")
2. There are twelve one-cent stamps in a dozen. How many two-cent stamps are in a dozen? (HINT: How many of anything are in a dozen?)
3. Use four straight lines to connect these nine dots *without* lifting your pencil from the paper. (Hint: Don't try to stay within the dots.)

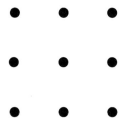

4. A father and a son are in a car accident. The father dies. The son is rushed to the emergency room. The surgeon on duty takes one look at the boy and says, "I can't operate on this boy. He's my son!" Can this be true?

(Answers to these riddles are on page 128.)

Brainteasers like these cause you to jump-shift your thinking, to make connections in ways your brain is not used to making them. Your library probably has books filled with brainteaser of all types. However, don't be afraid to make up your own on the spot. Proclaim your ability to walk on water. (Then slide across a frozen puddle.) Or exclaim "Now wait a minute. How could the basketball team have won last night? Not a single man on our side made a basket!" (It was the women's basketball team.) In no time, your child will be finding ways to stump you, too.

➤ Don't put away the blocks. The directions for the Lego spaceship might have long since disappeared, and the wooden building blocks might be gathering dust in the basement, but don't hand those classic building toys down to a younger cousin just yet. Instead, take those blocks out, dust them off, and place them in a fresh box or basket in the middle of the living room or in front of the television set.

Building is just plain fun. (If you need proof, set a small bowl of

Legos out the next time you entertain guests and watch what happens!)
Although the creations of a fourth grader will be different from the creations of a four-year-old or a civil engineer, the same skills in spatial problem solving apply. There are many, many construction toys in all sizes,
shapes, and materials on the market today, but the actual construction
materials are not important. Cardboard boxes work as well as anything
else. What *is* important is that while your child has fun, her confidence in
problem solving keeps building.

➤ Be a mathemagician. Amaze and astound your child with your wizardry,
and then show her how to do the same with her friends. Here is a trick to
get you started. Write it on a slip of paper and pull it out of your wallet
when you're in the dentist's waiting room. (You'll find plenty of other
tricks in puzzle books and magazines available at your library or bookstore.)

MAGIC NINES

Tell your child:
1. Write down a big number you know by heart (zip code, telephone
   number, birthdate).
   53711
2. Scramble the digits.
   11573
3. Subtract the smaller number from the larger number.
   $53,711 - 11,573 = 42,138$
4. Add up the digits in the answer.
   18
5. Add up the digits in *that* answer.
   9

Add-a-ca-da-bra! The answer is 9!

If your child is not strong in computation, let her use a calculator to
work the trick. The object is: *numbers are fun!*

➤ Remember that a little humor goes a long way. One of the most frustrat-
ing aspects of math—its vocabulary—can also be its most humorous.
Suppose the instructions in your child's math text say, "Reduce the fraction 18/54." Before starting in on the serious business of equivalent frac-

tions (more on that in Fractions, page 166), you might exclaim, "Hey, I can reduce any fraction in a second! Watch this!" and write,

$$\frac{18}{54} \quad \frac{18}{54} \quad \frac{18}{54} \quad \frac{18}{54} \quad \frac{18}{54}$$

Or maybe a multiple choice quiz says, "Which number comes between 4 and 500?" You tell your child, "Hey, I can count by ones from zero to a number between four and five hundred in just five seconds!" Then count from 0 to 5 and point out that 5 is definitely between 4 and 500.

Finally, don't forget measurement words, such as *long*, *wide*, and *square*. Some of the world's oldest jokes work on the humorous possibilities of these words:

Customer: "I need some long underwear."

Salesperson: "How long do you want it?"

Customer: "Oh, from about November to March."

HAVE MORE TIME?

➤ Play games. Playing games with your child is the "read to your child" of mathematics. The time you spend playing a card or board game with your child is pure gold. If you did nothing but play a game of Gin Rummy with your child each night (and let her keep score), you would probably reinforce more problem-solving skills than a whole week's worth of workbook pages. Most card and board games are swimming in mathematical concepts; however, what your child gains by playing games with you goes far beyond mathematical skill. For example:

• Your undivided attention.

• Practice in following directions.

• Skill in negotiation. ("You took your hands off." "I did not." "You did too!")

• Instruction in the grace of losing—and winning.

• Fun with Mom or Pop.

You might find that your fourth grader is on a game-playing cusp. She can play games like Checkers and Battleship with aplomb, strategically planning her next move; yet she is impatient and often plunges ahead without taking advantage of her skills in strategy. She denounces games like Go Fish and War as childish, yet she shies away from more difficult games like Gin Rummy or Hearts. The more you play with your child, the more willing she will be to stretch her horizons.

The games listed below are particularly useful in developing strategic and logical thinking. You can make homemade versions of many of these games with file folders or sheets of cardboard, paper, and buttons or coins to serve as markers. Also check your library for *Kids' Games,* by Phil Wiswell; *Games of the World,* by Frederick Grunfeld; or other books of children's games.

Backgammon	Chess	Othello
Battleship	Cribbage	Parcheesi
Card games of any sort	Go	Yote
Checkers	Mancala	

➤Suggest that your child make her own board game. You *know* you should be pleased that your child already knows every batting average in the National League by the age of nine, but there comes a time when the information itself wears a bit thin. Encourage your little fanatic to use her extraordinary knowledge to make a National League (or American Girls doll or Nintendo) board game. Help her check around the house for supplies. You might use the suggestions below, but don't underestimate your child's own inventiveness. Who knows what inspiration lies buried in the recycling bin or the junk drawer?

Game boards: file folders, cardboard boxes, paper bags, Styrofoam trays, egg cartons

Question cards: index cards, Post-it notes, old business or greeting cards

Markers: buttons, coins, Legos, index cards folded in half, spice bottles, empty film cans, large beads, old jewelry

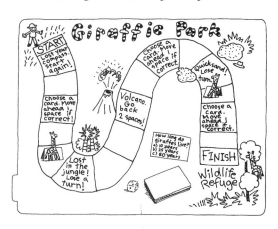

➤ Fourth graders are great planners. Take advantage of this delightful trait by giving your child responsibility for a big project. If you truly allow your child to take control from beginning to end, you will see some amazing problem-solving skills in action. Is your child a budding philanthropist? A junior entrepreneur? An avid environmentalist? Even if your child's idea is not as practical as you might wish ("We could go to every grocery store and tell them to stop selling meat!" says your young vegetarian), beware of naysaying too early. With a little thought and guidance, your child is bound to come up with a project that fits her interests. Here are a few conversation starters.

For humanitarians: start a toys and book drive for children at a homeless shelter; make cards or small gifts for residents of a nearby nursing home; get together a group of friends to read to children in a daycare center; put on a performance and donate ticket money to charity.

For entrepreneurs: set up a table in the front yard and sell homemade crafts; start a dog-walking business; put together a magic show and hire out to young children's birthday parties.

For environmentalists: start a recycling program at home, at school, or in the neighborhood; start a mini bird sanctuary in the backyard; adopt a stream or an endangered animal. The Audubon Society, your local librarian, or a search on the Internet can get you started.

For political activists: write letters to the president, the mayor, the school superintendent, the local newspaper; take a survey; collect signatures for a petition.

For more ideas, check out *Making Cents, Every Kid's Guide to Money* (Little, Brown) or *The Kid's Guide to Social Service Projects: Over 500 Service Ideas for Young People Who Want to Make a Difference*, by Barbara A. Lewis (Free Spirit Publishing).

➤ Draw. Or paint, or sculpt, or make collages, or make prints. The more time your child spends "messing about" in art, the more she is exploring geometry ("What shape is that? Is that side straight or slightly curved?"), algebra ("If I make the dinosaur this big, how big will the plants have to be?"), and number sense ("If I kept going like this, would it make a pattern?"). Moreover, drawing asks your child to use the same problem-solving skill that the logic games above do: the skill of looking at a problem from a different point of view.

➤ Play a new version of Tic-tac-toe. By now, there's a good chance that your sophisticated fourth grader has figured out the winning strategy to the classic three spaces by three spaces Tic-tac-toe game. Challenge her with something new. For each game, take turns placing *X*'s or *O*'s in the spaces.

ULTRA TIC-TAC-TOE

Use the squares on a checkerboard or sheet of graph paper. A player needs five in a row to win.

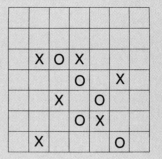

CANNONBALLS

Three in a row wins.

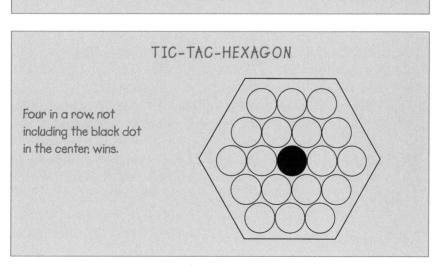

TIC-TAC-HEXAGON

Four in a row, not including the black dot in the center, wins.

Answers to math riddles

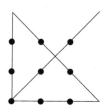

1. A nickel and a half dollar (only *one* is not a nickel).
2. Twelve, of course.
3. See figure at right for the solution.
4. The surgeon was the boy's *mother.*

Sharing Problem-Solving Strategies

Let's say you have three apples and four children. Knowing your children as you do, you assume that it is imperative to give each one an equal portion of apple. What are some ways you might go about solving your dilemma? You might:

- Guess and check.
- Draw a picture.
- Use objects or a model.
- Act it out.
- Look for a pattern.
- Construct a table.
- Do a simpler or similar problem.

Certain strategies work better for certain people. For example, if you find it easiest to solve problems that you can "see," you might find it easier to draw a picture or make a model. Some strategies work better for certain types of problems. Problems involving large numbers, for instance, often seem more manageable with the temporary substitution of smaller numbers. By giving your child a range of strategies from which to choose, you are increasing his flexibility and chances for success in problem solving.

HAVE FIVE MINUTES?

➤ Point out the problem-solving possibilities in everyday life.
- Rather than "I've told you a hundred times to put that backpack away!" try "How can we solve that backpack problem?"
- Rather than "Let's measure to see if that bookcase will fit there," try "Do you think that bookcase will fit there? How can we figure that out?"
- Rather than "If you watch any more television, you're going to turn into a zombie!" try "You're spending an awful lot of your free time in front of the TV. How can you have some TV time but still have time to do other things, too?"

➤ Problems in everyday life are often messy. Sometimes important information is missing. Sometimes the information is hidden among worthless details. Whenever your child is stuck on a problem, ask him where he needs to be on the problem-solving chart below. It will help keep him on track.

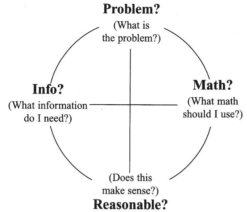

Problem?
(What is
the problem?)

Info?
(What information
do I need?)

Math?
(What math
should I use?)

(Does this
make sense?)
Reasonable?

Have your child answer the questions she knows the answers to. Then help her figure out the answers to the remaining questions.

➤Throw away your pencil and paper. Encourage your child to do math in his head. Think about the problem solving you do during the course of your day. How many times do you take out a pencil and paper to solve problems at home, in the office, or at the grocery store? Mental math demands a flexible approach to problem solving. When your child solves a problem in his head, he knows that his thinking is his own. The knowledge that he can solve problems on his own is the most precious intellectual gift you can give your child.

➤Encourage your child to come up with multiple solutions for the same problem: "Okay, your mom has the car and we want to get to the library. What are our options?" Your child may suggest walking, taking the bus, or waiting until later that afternoon.

➤List two or three seemingly dissimilar things, such as wind and water, and ask your child how the items are alike (both can shape the earth; both can be used as an energy source, and so on).

➤Introduce your child to the Amazing Transformation Machine. Explain that whenever you put something into the ATM, it is transformed into something else. Choose two or three items to put into the ATM and then have your child perform the transformation, for example,
  • "I put in three circles—"
    "—and a traffic light came out!"

- "I put in a quarter and a nickel—"
  "—and three dimes came out!"
- "I put in a chicken and a pig—"
  "—and I got breakfast!"

Be sure your child can explain what transformation took place. Then switch roles. You'll find that it's harder than you think!

HAVE MORE TIME?

➤ Play Seven to Eleven.

SEVEN TO ELEVEN

1. Use nine red cards and nine black cards from a deck of cards. Write on a piece of paper, "There are 2 more black cards in the long row than red cards in the short row." Place the piece of paper in a sealed envelope.
2. Tell your child that you can predict the future—in fact, you have predicted the outcome to this trick. Give your child the sealed envelope.
3. Hand your child the eighteen cards to shuffle.
4. Tell him to deal the cards face up in two rows *in any order he wants.* There should be seven cards in the first row and eleven in the second row.
5. Finally, have your child open the envelope. Wow, are you amazing!

Challenge your child to figure out how you did the trick. [Do *you* know the secret to this trick? Take the difference between the number of cards in the first row and the number in the second row (11 − 7 = 4). Then divide that difference by 2 (4 ÷ 2 = 2). The resulting number is how many more black cards there will be in the long row than reds in the short row (or more reds in the long row than blacks in the short row)]. To prove the secret, try placing the cards in rows of six or twelve. The difference between the two rows is 6. Half of that is 3. Now count your cards. Are there three more black cards in the long row than reds in the short row and three more reds in the long row than there are in the short row? As long as you use the same number of red cards and black cards, the trick should work for any number of cards in any length of rows! You can find books with more card tricks in your library or book store.

➤ Teach your child Nine Men's Morris. Many different cultures have versions of this ancient game. Originally, the game was probably played with stones on a board drawn in the dirt. You can draw your board on a sheet of paper. Each player also needs a set of nine markers, such as red and black checkers or dimes and pennies. Here's how to play.

NINE MEN'S MORRIS

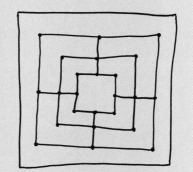

1. To start, take turns placing one marker on any of the twenty-four points on the board. Continue until all eighteen markers are placed on the board.
2. Take turns sliding your markers along the board lines to any open point on the board. Jumping is not allowed, and no two markers can share one point at the same time.
3. Continue to move your markers until you get three markers in a horizontal or vertical (not diagonal) row, called a *mill*. A mill entitles you to remove one of your opponent's pieces from the board. You may remove any marker *except* one that is already part of a mill (three in a row).
4. A player wins when his opponent has only two pieces left or cannot move.

➤ Play Stump the Parent. Have your child use the newspaper, the *Guinness Book of World Records,* or an almanac to create problems for you to solve. Here's one example: "It takes 5,670,000 bloodsucking banded lice to make one ounce. How many of these insects would it take to make a pound?"

➤ Use an outline map of the United States to give your child this challenge: "Use only four colors. Can you color each state a different color from the one bordering it?" Play with different maps or designs to see if you or your junior cartographer can find one that requires *more* than four colors.

Modeling Persistence and Spunk

Psssst. Your child is watching. Here's the scenario. It's a cold morning. You go out to start the car. You turn the key. The car whirs. You turn the key again.

It whirs again (well, maybe this time it's more like a groan). Then it just clicks. What do you do?

Right. You fuss or fume. Or perhaps you kick or curse. But after that, you probably problem solve. Exactly how you problem solve might depend upon any number of factors: how much time you have, your automotive expertise, the tools you have handy, other transportation means available to you, friends or neighbors you can count on, how important your mission in the outside world is. One way or another, however, you solve the problem. This is what your child sees.

When people talk about math fear or math anxiety, they are talking about being afraid to *approach* a problem. People who are anxious about math tend to say "I can't" or "I don't know how" before they ever get started. Much of this attitude has been perpetuated by the way math has been taught. Many children come to believe that there is a formula for every problem and if they don't know the formula, they can't do the problem. Yet, think about the best problem solvers you know. Do they rely on formulas? More likely, their problem-solving skills are surprisingly nonarithmetical: skills like patience, persistence, concentration, and tolerance of failure. Teaching these habits is not as easy as teaching your child to "subtract the ones column first." No matter how hard you try, you cannot force a child to be persistent any more than you can force her to be happy. But you can create an environment where persistence, concentration, and a "never say die" attitude can flourish."

Listen Actively

By taking the time and energy to go beyond a distracted "Um-hum," you show your child that you appreciate and respect how she thinks. Even if your child's answer to a problem seems totally off the wall, remember that something about it makes sense to her. Careful listening does not have to be time-consuming, but it does take some practice. The "one-liners" below might help you get started.

- "How did you get that?" Even if your child is completely confused, there is bound to be one small part of her explanation that is accurate or makes sense to you. That little bit is your starting point for discussion.
- "Hey! That's the answer I got! Let's compare how we got our answers."
- "I don't know. How can we figure this out?" The urge to tell or show your child how to do something is an instinctive part of parenting. In mathematics, at least, do your very best to block that urge. Telling your child how to get the right answer may be expedient in the short term. In the long term, however, your child might have missed another opportunity to see herself as a capable, flexible, successful problem solver.

HAVE FIVE MINUTES?

➤Accept wrong answers. "Yikes!" you might say. "But isn't accuracy the whole point of mathematics?" Of course, accuracy is important in math; but the correlation is not necessarily that inaccuracy is a sin. Mathematical skill and confidence come not from magically hitting upon the answer but from *figuring out* the answer, often after many false starts or unsuccessful attempts. When you say, "Hmm, how did you go about getting that answer?" rather than "Nope. That's wrong," you are giving your child a chance to take a risk, examine her own results, and come up with a solution on her own. Look for what your child is doing right and build on that. Don't worry; the right answers will follow. Children like to be right.

➤ Let your child be the teacher. It's a rare child who doesn't get some pleasure out of catching her parent in a mistake. Every now and then, when you're paying bills, or buying groceries, or planning a home improvement project, ask your child to double-check your math. If there's an error—and it's always more fun if there is—ask your child to explain to you what you did wrong. In the process, she will be strengthening her own problem-solving skills.

➤ Make up a code. Solving a code takes persistence. Making one up takes even more persistence. The Two Wrongs Make a Right Code, below, will get you both started. Then see if you can make up others to stump each other while you wait in the doctor's or dentist's office.

$$\begin{array}{r} \text{WRONG} \\ + \text{WRONG} \\ \hline \text{Right} \end{array}$$

(HINT: Try G = 1, N = 8, R = 7)

The book *Key to the Treasure,* by Peggy Parish, has inspired children toward code-making and solving for years. If your child hasn't already read the book, now's the time to check it out of the library.

If you run out of inspiration, you might also take a peek at one of the hundreds of codebooks available. A few particularly good ones for fourth graders are

- *Pass It On! All About Notes, from Secret Codes and Special Inks to Fancy Folds and Dead Man's Drops,* by Sharon Bailly (Millbrook Press)
- *Secret Codes: Science Action Book,* by Robert Jackson (Running Press)
- *The Usborne Book of Secret Codes,* by Eileen O'Brien and Diana Riddell (EDC Press)

HAVE MORE TIME?

➤ Encourage your child to pursue a hobby, take up a musical instrument, or learn a sport. Building a model airplane, learning to play "Frere

Jacques," figuring out how to stay upright on a pair of skis, and solving a math problem all require the same habits of mind: determination, concentration, and stick-with-it-ness. One word of warning: *Be very wary of overbooking your child.* Most fourth graders are at least temporarily interested in just about anything that comes their way. The line between encouraging interests and spreading your child too thin is indeed very difficult to draw. The following suggestions may help.

- Limit your child's outside activities. The exact number is a highly individual choice. Remember, however, that exploration and resourcefulness and persistence all take time—uninterrupted time—and space. Give your child a chance to be a child, to play, even if it means having to schedule in "unscheduled" time!
- Agree on a time commitment for each activity. Your child might decide that she would really rather build a birdhouse than do a needlepoint for Gran's birthday, or she might discover that her best friend isn't going to be on the ice hockey team after all and therefore she'd rather not play. Agreeing on a time commitment *beforehand* ("Okay, try the saxophone for one term, and if you decide you want to switch to drums after that, you can") might help your child get past a momentary flagging of interest or a rocky start.
- Observe your child carefully. Some fourth graders will push themselves until they drop, while others carry on about real and imagined injuries as though they were miniature Camilles. Only you can decide whether your child's sudden droopiness means that your child is overextended or a hypochondriac. If you've been watching carefully, most likely you'll make the right call.

➤ Give your child control over her own money—either in the form of an allowance or as payment for household jobs well done. There are few times when a child is more motivated and persistent than when she wants to buy something. And when the money she is spending is her own, you can bet that she will problem solve with agility and ingenuity.

➤ Work on a *big* problem. Mathematicians have been working on seemingly unsolvable problems since time began. Look in the *Guinness Book of World Records* and you will probably find that someone has discovered a few new decimal places for the irrational number pi. (At last count, it has been calculated to over 6 billion decimal places!) Keep your eye out for never-ending problems, and tack one up on the refrigerator every so often. Here are a couple to get you and your family started:

- If $a = 1¢$, $b = 2¢$, and so on to $z = 26¢$, how many words can you think of that equal one dollar?

- Can you trace this figure without lifting your finger (or pencil) off the paper? You may cross over lines, but you may not retrace any lines. (For the solution to this, see page 136.)

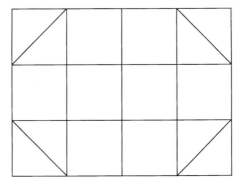

Number Sense

The ability to understand number is measured by questions 1 to 5 and 17 on the Math Assessment.

Number sense is one of those terms that is bandied about the educational community. Parents, administrators, and even teachers themselves *sort of* know what it means: "It's everything besides computation, right?" "It's learning about big numbers and that stuff, right?"

Number sense is, in fact, the "common sense" of mathematics. If a store clerk were to charge you $7.13 for two items costing 25¢ and 78¢, you might say to yourself (and to him), "Hmm, that doesn't seem right." If, in response, the clerk were to recalculate and come up with exactly the same total, you might be moved to shout, "Use a little common sense, would you?" That common sense about numbers and how they work is what number sense is all about.

Long before your child ever started school, he had already acquired a great deal of number sense simply by trying to make sense out of the world around him—by noticing patterns, by counting and recounting objects, by figuring out that Mom's big hand can hold more raisins than his little hand. Unfortunately, your child's past four or five years of formal math instruction has not necessarily guaranteed a more advanced sense of number. Indeed, the exact opposite might be true. For too many children, learning formal computation techniques actually detracts from their natural sense of number. When your child concludes that 25 + 78 = 713 or that 1/2 + 1/2 = 2/4, he might be making a valiant effort to learn a computation method. Unfortunately, in the process, he is leaving his number sense behind.

Without a solid sense of how numbers work, even a student who is highly skilled in computation will begin to struggle as he tries to pile ever more complex mathematical concepts onto his shaky foundation. To develop an intuitive understanding of number, your fourth grader needs to have lots of opportunities to experience number.

- By recognizing and playing with patterns.
- By estimating quantities and sizes.
- By strengthening his understanding of place value.
- By exploring different types of numbers and their relationships to each other.

Like common sense, number sense is difficult to learn in a classroom setting. Only plenty of common, everyday experiences will give your child an understanding of how numbers make sense. And only you have the time and opportunity to make those experiences happen.

Playing with Patterns

All mathematics is about patterns—about noticing what is the same and what is different in different situations and using that understanding to solve problems. Your child has been noticing patterns from the moment he first discovered the striped socks covering his infant toes. Luckily, patterns are all around you—in tree leaves and playground chants, in window frames and carpet designs, on license plates and street numbers—and as your child gets older, pattern finding becomes more challenging and interesting. If the patterns of rhythm and rhyme in "Mary Had a Little Lamb" seem babyish, how about a Bach fugue? For additional activities involving patterns, see Geometry, page 169.

Answer to puzzle on page 135.

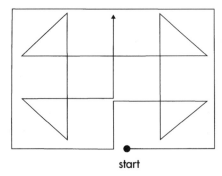

start

➤Point out the patterns around you, especially those that are not really apparent. It might be easy to pick out the pattern in the kitchen floor tiles, but what about that ugly carpet on the stairs? How about the tree opposite the bus stop? Do its branches form a pattern, or do they seem to grow at random? How about that obnoxious ditty that's stuck in your head? Does it have a pattern? Would it be a little less annoying if it *didn't* have a pattern (and would it stick in your head)?

➤Make number soup. On a magnetic board or a piece of paper taped to the refrigerator, draw a large circle. Inside the circle, place three or four numbers that follow a pattern. Challenge your child to find the rule to the pattern. To do this, he can either guess new numbers, which you place either inside the "soup" (circle) or outside, or he can take a stab at the rule itself ("All are numbers divisible by ten"). Make a new number soup each day. As your child gets used to looking for patterns, throw a tricky one in here or there, such as the one below. (In case you're stumped, the answer is on page 141.)

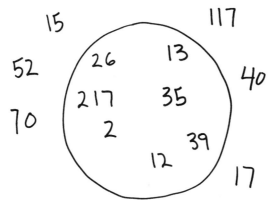

➤Look for patterns in numbers. Does your zip code contain a pattern? How about your telephone number? Today's date? What about your child's birthday or the registration number on his bicycle?

➤Need to stop a squabble in the backseat? Start a number sequence. Give your child two numbers—say, 1 and 2—and challenge him to continue the sequence in as many ways as possible. For example, you say, "One, two . . . " and he says, "Four, eight, sixteen . . . I multiplied by two. Three, four, five . . . I added one." Any sequence is acceptable, as long as your child can give you the rule behind it.

➤ Got a restless kid? See how fast he can body count. Body counting—touching different parts of the body in a specific sequence—is actually an art in New Guinea. Use the sequence below or challenge your child to make up one of his own.

1. Right little finger
2. Right ring finger
3. Right middle finger
4. Right index finger
5. Right thumb
6. Right wrist
7. Right elbow
8. Right shoulder
9. Right ear
10. Right eye
11. Mouth
12. Left eye
13. Left ear
14. Left shoulder
15. Left elbow

HAVE MORE TIME?

➤ Treat your child to a display of Nimble Nines. The number 9 has fascinated people for thousands of years—even non-nine-year-olds! The ancient Greeks used the number 9 as a symbol of indestructibility. Perhaps after witnessing a few of its amazing feats, your child will think it's indestructible, too!

1. List the multiplication table for 9, as shown at right. Ask your child to point out any patterns he sees. (For example, the products of 9×6 through 9×10 are transposed versions of the products of 9×5 through 9×1.)
2. Ask your child to add the digits of each product together. What does he notice? (They each add up to 9.) Now ask your child to multiply a large

$9 \times 379 = 3411$ $3 + 4 + 1 + 1 = 9$

$9 \times 641 = 5769$ $5 + 7 + 6 + 9 = 27$ $2 + 7 = 9$

number by 9 and add the digits together until he gets a one-digit number. What number is it?
3. Show your child a calendar. Circle any 3×3 square of numbers, as shown. Ask your child to multiply the center number by 9 ($9 \times 10 = 90$).

$9 \times 1 = 9$

$9 \times 2 = 18$

$9 \times 3 = 27$

$9 \times 4 = 36$

$9 \times 5 = 45$

$9 \times 6 = 54$

$9 \times 7 = 63$

$9 \times 8 = 72$

$9 \times 9 = 81$

$9 \times 10 = 90$

Then ask him to add up all nine of the circled numbers. What is the sum? The trick will work with any 3 × 3 boxes on the calendar.

Sunday	Monday	Tuesday	Wednesday	Thursday	Friday	Saturday
	1	2	3	4	5	6
7	8	9	10	11	12	13
14	15	16	17	18	19	20
21	22	23	24	25	26	27
28	29	30				

➤ Create a clapping or Hacky-sack routine. Chances are, your fourth grader has probably already picked up a few routines, or at least the eloquent lyrics that accompany them:

Three, six, nine, the rooster drank wine.
The monkey chewed tobacco on a streetcar line.
The streetcar broke, the monkey got choked.
And they all went to heaven in a little rowboat. Oh, yeah!

Suggest that your child make up a new routine, with or without an accompanying rhyme. Then see if you are adept enough to follow the pattern!

➤ Look for patterns in pairs of numbers. Your child has actually been doing this for years: one person has two legs, two people have four legs, three people have six legs, and so on. Show your child how to record these patterns in table form.

Erasers	Price	Baseball Teams	Players
1	25¢	1	9
2	50¢	2	18
3	75¢	3	27
4	$1.00	4	
5			

➤Play a pattern memory game. Make or draw a sequence and show it to your child. Allow your child to view the pattern for a set time—say, ten seconds. Take the pattern away and ask your child to draw or describe the next three items in the pattern. After your child has succeeded in continuing a sequence correctly, switch roles.

Estimating

Estimating is one of the most sense-making activities we do. How do you figure out if you have enough time to eat breakfast before leaving for work? Or if your car can fit in the for-compact-cars-only space in the parking garage? Or if you'll need to go to the bank before you can pay the baby-sitter tonight? You estimate. Research shows that most adults use estimation to solve nearly *half* of the mathematical problems that pop up during the course of their day.

For your child to make sense out of numbers, she needs to know what is a reasonable amount and what is not. According to recent research, however, most students are reluctant to estimate an answer to a problem *even when an exact answer is impossible or unnecessary.* Children like to be right. Many hate estimating simply because it seems so inexact. Moreover, many math programs support these attitudes by emphasizing pencil-and-paper computation methods that lead to one right answer.

This year, your child will be computing with numbers that go into the hundred thousands. She will be comparing fractions and figuring out where to put the point in a decimal problem. As the numbers your child works with grow larger and more complex, the ability to figure out whether or not they are reasonable becomes increasingly critical. By practicing estimation with your child whenever you can, you will be helping her develop the good sense that is crucial to her success in mathematics.

HAVE FIVE MINUTES?

➤Estimate, estimate. Estimating is a great time-passer. How many feet are in this line of people? How many goals can you kick in five minutes? How many glasses will fit in the dishwasher? How long can you stand on one leg? How much is this meal going to cost? Take a few moments to share and compare the reasoning behind each of your estimates.

➤Get into the habit of asking your child "Estimate or exact?" whenever questions of quantity or measurement come up: How much time does your child need for homework? Will her library books fit in her backpack? How much money should she take for the bake sale? Does she need to wear a jacket today? Point out times when an approximate answer is as good as, or even better than, an exact answer.

➤ Talk about benchmarks. Think back to the last time you tried to estimate the number of people in a crowd. How many people were at the game last night: 15,000? 30,000? 45,000? Would it help if you knew that the stadium held 50,000 people and that it was almost full? Relating estimates to something you already know usually improves your chance of coming up with a reasonable guess. If your child is trying to estimate how many books are in her bookcase, it might help her to think first about the number of books on one shelf.

➤ Get into the habit of rounding off numbers. This year, your child will be expected to know how to round numbers to the nearest thousand. Be sure that your child knows the steps for rounding up or down:

Rounding Up to the Nearest Thousand

1. Find the digit in the thousands place: **16,**845.
2. Look at the digit to the right of it: 16,**8**45.
3. If the digit is 5 or greater, round up adding 1 to the digit in the thousands place. Change all the digits to the right of the rounded digit to zeros: **17,000.**

Rounding Down to the Nearest Thousand

1. Find the digit in the thousands place: **8,**347.
2. Look at the digit to the right of it: 8,**3**47.
3. If the digit is less than 5, the digit in the thousands place stays the same. Change all the digits to the right of the rounded digit to zeros: **8,000.**

Point out exact numbers in the news or in daily conversation. Ask "Would it make sense to use a rounded number here? What would that number be?"

➤ Ask your child "About how many breaths do you think you take in a minute? In a day? In a week? How about in a year?" Talk about different strategies you might use to make and check the estimations.

Answer to number soup example:
   All of the numbers begin with the letter *T*.

HAVE MORE TIME?

➤ Have fun with wild estimates. Even if you manage to convince your child that there are times when estimation is useful, she still might be hesitant to leave the security of one right answer. Help your child come up with a list of weird or wild estimation quiz questions. Write your estimates down and then talk about ways you might go about checking your estimation. You might learn some interesting bits of information, and your child will learn that being "way off" is not the worst thing in the world that can happen. The following questions might spark some ideas. Check your estimates in the *Guinness Book of World Records*.

- How much money does the richest person in the world have?
- How many words are in an unabridged dictionary?
- How old was the youngest student ever to attend a university?
- How many stories tall is the world's tallest house of cards?

➤ If your child has difficulty remembering the rules for rounding numbers to the nearest ten, you might offer this visual support. Fold a strip of paper in an accordion fold and lay it on the table so that it forms a series of peaks and valleys. Label each peak and valley as shown.

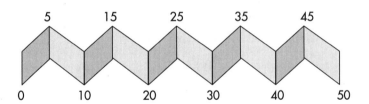

Place a marble or other small object at about 17 and watch it slide down to the 20. Ask what would happen if you placed the marble at 33. (It would slide down to 30.) Repeat the process, using numbers in the hundreds and thousands. Remind your child that a marble placed on the very top of a peak (5, 50, 500) always rolls to the higher number.

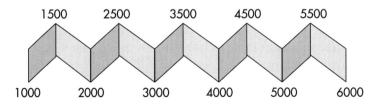

➤ Ask your fourth grader to help with menu planning and grocery list writing. Do you have enough cheese for tacos? How much rice do you need for four people? Will one eggplant do for eggplant parmigiana? And make sure you give your child plenty of opportunities to help with the cooking as well. The time she spends practicing estimation will be well worth the kitchen mess.

➤ Make headline news. Read aloud statistics that you come across in newspapers or magazines. Ask your child to make up a headline using the information. Talk about whether an estimate or an exact figure is needed in each case.

Understanding Place Value

In some ways, the standard mathematics curriculum has parents and teachers in a bind. They instinctively know (as do their charges!) that certain operations in addition and subtraction are "way harder" than other operations in multiplication and division. Yet, without the standard benchmarks—addition in first grade, subtraction in second, multiplication in third, division in fourth, fractions in fifth, decimals in sixth—how do you know what to teach or how your child is doing? On the other hand, what do you do with the fourth grader who has his addition, subtraction, multiplication, and division facts down cold but still adds 87 and 76 and comes up with 1,513?

You go back to place value. The fourth grader above is probably a very good math student. Unfortunately, he has learned his addition and subtraction as a series of computational tricks and now lacks the true understanding to move on. Place value is more than just being able to read the numeral 154,683,245 aloud. It is the very basis of how we understand numbers and compute within our number system.

Our base-ten place value system is so central to an understanding of the way numbers work that even children with strong computational skills will benefit from activities that strengthen place value concepts. This year, your child will be multiplying large numbers with zeros in them, estimating quotients in division, and computing with decimals. To move forward in mathematics with confidence, he will need to be able to move around the base-ten system with ever-increasing agility.

HAVE FIVE MINUTES?

➤ Reading large numbers is often thought to be more difficult than it actually is. To read numbers in the millions or even the billions, all your child has to know is how to read three-digit numbers (as in 365) and the names of the *periods*—that is, the thousands, millions, billions, and so on. Turn a sheet of notebook paper sideways and mark the periods, as shown. Don't forget the commas between the periods! Then write numbers in each column and ask your child to practice reading the various numbers aloud.

Trillions	Billions	Millions	Thousands	
000,	000,	000,	000,	000
	21,	755,	803,	122

Practice, Practice

Keep working on addition and subtraction. The more comfortable your child is shifting ones and tens and hundreds about, the easier multiplication, division, and decimal computations are bound to be.

- Teach your child how to do "comparative shopping." Ask him to tell you which brand or which store has the cheaper price for the same item and by how much. Talk about why you might or might not buy the cheaper item.
- Ask your child to estimate, then figure out, the total order at a restaurant.
- Use an outdoor thermometer or weather reports to keep a weather chart listing the daily high and low temperature. Use the chart to ask questions such as "How much warmer was it today than yesterday?" or "What was the difference between yesterday's low and high temperatures?"

➤ Whenever you are driving, play License Plate Top-It. Take turns reading license plates as numbers (excluding the letters). For example, 737R562 would read as seven hundred thirty-seven thousand, five hundred sixty-two. Each player must find and read a number that is greater than the previous one.

➤ Show your child how to write a number in expanded notation (also known as expanded form). Expanded notation is simply another way to show a number. In expanded notation the number 5,286 is expressed as

$$5000 + 200 + 80 + 6.$$

Give your child numbers to write out or tell you in expanded form. Then switch roles. See who can stump the other. (HINT: numbers with zeros in them, such as 101,068, are the hardest.)

➤ Play Estimation Beats the Calculator. With your child, make a list of large number addition and subtraction problems. Ask your child to estimate the answer to each problem as you enter the exact numbers into the calculator. See who comes up with an *answer* first.

➤ Establish a daily friendly competition. See who can find the largest number in the morning newspaper and read it aloud.

➤Talk out loud about how you use rounding and your understanding of place value to figure out problems in your head. For example, you might say, "You know how I figured that out so fast? I thought, 'Well, 599 is just one less than 600, so I added 600 instead of 599 and then just took one away.'"

HAVE MORE TIME?

➤The more ways your child deals with the concept of place value, the better he will understand it. If your child struggles when working with larger numbers, additional experience with concrete objects (called "manipulatives" in educationese) might help him sort out his confusion. Objects such as base-ten blocks show your child that one ten is actually the same size (or equal to) ten ones, and that one hundred is the same size as ten tens.

You can purchase base-ten blocks at most toy or teaching supply stores, or use the patterns below to make your own out of cardboard or plastic sheets. Start out by asking your child to "build" various numbers with the fewest blocks possible. Then suggest that he use the blocks whenever he is stumped on an addition or subtraction problem.

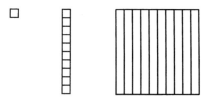

The number 342 would then be represented by three flats, four longs, and two units:

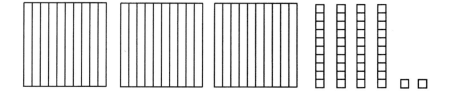

➤Try chip or stick trading. If your fourth grader has used base-ten blocks throughout his early elementary school years, he might decide that he is "past" using manipulatives. In fact, he might be half right—base-ten blocks have not done the trick. This does not mean, however, that he doesn't need concrete experience—he just needs something new. Try using a set of poker chips or trading sticks to represent ones, tens, and hundreds in a slightly more abstract version of base-ten blocks. Your child can make trading sticks by coloring the tips of craft sticks these colors: yellow, blue, green, and red.

Whichever manipulatives you use, designate one color for each place value. Make a chart as shown and ask your child to use the manipulatives to show various numbers and to solve addition and subtraction problems.

Challenge: show 342.

GREEN	RED	YELLOW	BLUE
(Thousands)	(Hundreds)	(Tens)	(Ones)

➤ Play Grab the Buck. To play, you need two dice or number cubes and a pile of play money from a board game such as Monopoly. You can also make your own money out of slips of paper. You'll need about twenty of each denomination. Here's how to play:

GRAB THE BUCK

1. Decide on a low and high range, depending upon the play money you have. For example, you can play with $1's, $10's, and $100's; or with $100's, $1,000's and $10,000's.
2. In turn, each player rolls the dice and takes that number of the smallest denomination from the bank. For example, if a player is playing $100, $1,000, and $10,000 and rolls a 9, he takes $900 from the bank.
3. If a player has more than ten of any denomination (say, ten $100 bills), he *must* trade them in to the bank for the higher denomination (one $1,000 bill). If he does not, he forfeits one turn.
4. Play continues until one player can trade for the highest denomination (in this case, one $10,000 bill). The first player to "grab the buck" wins.

➤ Play Count Down. For this game, you need two dice or number cubes and pencil and paper.

COUNT DOWN

1. Make a score sheet with "1,000" at the top of each column.
2. The first player rolls the dice and makes a two-digit number from the numbers shown (for example, a roll of 6 and 3 could make 36 or 63).
3. Players alternate rolling the die, making a number, and subtracting the new number from their totals.
4. Play continues until one player cannot subtract his number without going below zero and the other player wins. You may start and end at any number. If your child needs addition practice, start low (at, say, 100) and end high (at 1,000).

Exploring Numbers and Their Relationships

Contrary to most fourth graders' basic belief, numbers do make sense. They fall into natural patterns and are highly predictable—so predictable, in fact, that throughout history certain numbers have been seen as magical.

Your child already knows a great deal about the nature of whole numbers. She probably knows if a number is odd or even, if it can be evenly divided by ten, and if a certain operation, such as addition or subtraction, will make the number larger or smaller. As she moves into more complex operations, such as long division and fraction computation, she will need an increasingly more sophisticated understanding of number: whether the number is prime or composite, what its factors and multiples are, and how different operations are related to each other. You can help your child gain this understanding by giving her plenty of practice in:

1. Recognizing equivalence ($3 = 1 + 2 = 120 \div 40 = 1/3$ of 9).
2. Exploring how operations are related to each other.

Here's how:

HAVE FIVE MINUTES?

➤ Point out the usefulness of knowing related facts, or *fact families*. By fourth grade, most students know their addition and multiplication facts cold, but many still stumble on subtraction and division facts. When your child draws a blank, give her a gentle nudge by reminding her of a related fact that she already knows. As soon as your child realizes that by knowing $7 \times 9 = 63$ she automatically knows the answers to 9×7, $63 \div 7$, and $63 \div 9$, she will definitely feel the power of families!

➤ Is everybody lined up outside the bathroom door early in the morning? Name a number. Then see how many other names for the same number you can come up with before Big Sis (or Dad or Junior) finally comes out of the bathroom. Names can include sums, differences, products, quotients, Roman numerals, fractions, tallies, and so on.

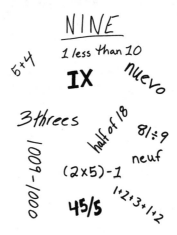

➤ Whenever you are traveling—even to the grocery store—suggest a number scavenger hunt. See how many of a certain type of number your child and you can find before you reach your destination. Here are a few suggestions:
- Multiples of 3.
- Prime numbers.
- Two numbers that can be put together in some way to make 10 (or 100, or 1,000).

➤ Point out and read Roman numerals wherever you find them—in books, on buildings and monuments, in movie credits, on clocks.

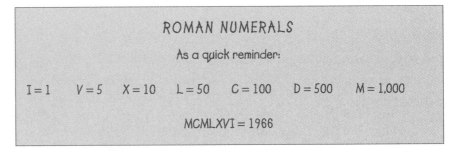

ROMAN NUMERALS

As a quick reminder:

I = 1   V = 5   X = 10   L = 50   C = 100   D = 500   M = 1,000

MCMLXVI = 1966

Number Lingo

Know and use the vocabulary of numbers whenever possible: "Our room's on the seventeenth floor. Hey! That's a prime number!" Here's a quick cheat sheet, in case you need it.

$$
\begin{array}{ccc}
\text{addend} & \text{minuend} & \text{factor} \\
\underline{+ \text{ addend}} & \underline{- \text{ subtrahend}} & \underline{\text{x factor}} \\
\text{sum} & \text{difference} & \text{product}
\end{array}
$$

$$
\overset{\text{quotient + remainder}}{\text{divisor}\,\overline{)\,\text{dividend}}}
$$

A **multiple** of a number is the product of that number and any other number. Multiples of 5 are 5, 10, 15, 20, 25, 30, 35, 40, and on and on.

A **factor** is a number that divides into another number evenly (with no remainder). The factors of 12 are 1, 2, 3, 4, 6, and 12.

A **prime number** is a number with only two factors: itself and 1. The numbers 2, 3, 5, 7, 11, 13, and 17 are all prime numbers.

A **square number** is the product of a number times itself. The numbers 9 (3×3), 16 (4×4), and 25 (5×5) are square numbers.

HAVE MORE TIME?

➤ While you are waiting (and waiting—and waiting) for your food in a restaurant, play the Disappearing Parent. Use a pencil to draw a simple geographic picture of yourself. Fill the body parts with random numbers. Tell your child that she can make her parent disappear simply by giving a different name for each number. (For instance, the Roman numeral M would make the right arm disappear below.) Names can include calculations, Roman numerals, fractions, drawings, and so on. Each time your child comes up with a name for one of the numbers, erase that part of the body. Can your child make you disappear before the food comes?

➤ Teach your child Name a Number Solitaire. This game not only keeps your child occupied at opportune moments, it reinforces the idea that a number can be named in several different ways.

NUMBER SOLITAIRE

1. Remove the face cards from the deck. Aces count as 1.
2. Shuffle the cards. Deal two cards face up on the table and place the rest of the pile face down in front of you.
3. Turn over the top card of the pile. If adding, subtracting, multiplying, or dividing the numbers on the face-up cards makes a fact with the number on top of the pile, take all three cards and set them aside. For instance, if you have the numbers 4 and 6, and you turn over a 10, you can make this fact: 4 + 6 = 10. If not, move the card from the pile to the table next to the other cards.
4. Turn over the next card and repeat the process. You may use only two cards from the table to make a fact with the card on the pile. For example, suppose 10, 3, 5, and 2 are face up on the table and you turn over a 7. You can use either 10 − 3 or 5 + 2 to make a fact with 7, but not both. The other two cards must remain on the table.
5. If there are no face-up cards on the table, the next card is from the pile (and, of course, the following one) automatically placed on the table.
6. Players try to have as few cards remaining on the table after the pile has been played as possible.

➤ Is 31 a prime number? How about 41? How about 51? Here's a game that will help take the trickiness out of recognizing prime numbers.

PRIME NUMBERS

1. Choose a small number, such as 6. Cut six small squares out of paper or use six square blocks or tiles.
2. Ask your child to use the squares to make a rectangle.
3. Then ask your child if she can make a second rectangle out of the squares. The rectangles will look like this:

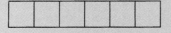

4. Repeat the process with the numbers 2 through 10. Keep a record of which numbers can make only one rectangle. These are the prime numbers.
5. Play around with different numbers. (Use graph paper for larger numbers.) Look for other patterns, such as square numbers or common multiples.

Multiplication

The ability to multiply whole numbers is measured by questions 1, 2, 6, and 7 on the Math Assessment.

Traditionally, the big push in multiplication begins in third grade. By fourth grade, your child will have probably been building arrays and memorizing times tables and answering questions about how many wheels there are on seven semi-trucks for quite a while. You might think that it's time to put multiplication behind you and move on to division.

In truth, most fourth graders still have a lot of multiplication to learn. The concepts and skills begun in third grade (or, in some cases, earlier) will continue to be built upon throughout fourth, fifth, and even sixth grade, including:

- Understanding the practical uses and different models of multiplication.
- Memorizing the multiplication facts to the point of instant recall.
- Multiplying by multiples of ten.
- Multiplying by one-, two-, and three-digit numbers.

Methods for teaching mathematics have always been the subject of much controversy. Today, many teachers and mathematicians feel that the traditional emphasis on paper and pencil calculation methods (90 percent of the child's math time, by some estimates) is outdated. In a world of computers and calculators, they maintain, children need to spend less time learning specific calculation methods and more time learning how to approach problems analytically and creatively. Even in classrooms where children are being encouraged to invent and share their own procedures for solving problems, however, chances are still very good that most fourth graders will be taught one of these following multiplication methods. **Be sure to find out which method your child is learning at school.** Failure to do so will only lead to additional confusion for your child.

1. Standard U.S. Algorithm (probably the one you learned in school):

$$
\begin{array}{r}
37 \\
\times 2 \\
\hline
74
\end{array}
\; (2 \times 7, \text{ then } 3 \times 2 + 1)
\qquad
\begin{array}{r}
37 \\
\times 42 \\
\hline
74 \\
1480 \\
\hline
1554
\end{array}
\begin{array}{l}
(2 \times 37) \\
(40 \times 37)
\end{array}
$$

2. Partial Products Algorithm (multiplies the larger numbers first):

$$
\begin{array}{r}
37 \\
\times 2 \\
\hline
60 \\
14 \\
\hline
74
\end{array}
\begin{array}{l}
(2 \times 30) \\
(2 \times 7)
\end{array}
\qquad
\begin{array}{r}
37 \\
\times 42 \\
\hline
1200 \\
280 \\
60 \\
14 \\
\hline
1554
\end{array}
\begin{array}{l}
(40 \times 30) \\
(40 \times 7) \\
(2 \times 30 \\
(2 \times 7)
\end{array}
$$

If your child is struggling in multiplication, observe him carefully as he works out a standard computation problem. Does he stumble over certain multiplication facts, such as the 7's, 8's, or 9's? Or does he seem confused about exactly how the computation method (or *algorithm*, as it is known in many programs) actually works? Do his numbers seem to dance all over the page, causing careless errors? Knowing your child's stumbling blocks will help you choose activities that will best support him in his struggle.

One last note: Quizzing your child on multiplication facts is not a sin, particularly if he enjoys the challenge. The sooner your child has those facts under his belt, the easier his life will be. Just remember to keep the quizzing lighthearted and stop before it reaches the point of tedium.

HAVE FIVE MINUTES?

➤If your child is struggling with memorizing his times tables, make sure that he knows the following shortcuts:

- Any number times 1 equals the original number.
- To find 2 times a number, double the number.
- To find 10 times a number, add a 0 to the end of the number ($7 \times 10 = $ **70**).
- When you multiply by 9, the first number in the answer is always 1 less than the number you are multiplying by ($9 \times$ **7** = **6**3).
- When you multiply by 9, the two numbers in the answer always add up to 9 ($9 \times 7 =$ **63**; $6 + 3 =$ **9**).

➤Does your child know his times tables but just takes a while to come up with the answers? Old-fashioned timed drills were not bad in concept—instant recall of facts makes all of the rest of math (and life) much easier—but they were *so boring*. Beyond that, fourth graders tend to be worriers who do not do well in timed tests. Here are some kinder, more lively ways you can help your child over the math facts hump.

- Play Hot Potato. Call out a fact as you toss a ball, beanbag, or pillow (or potato, for that matter!) to your child. He must give the answer before he catches the "potato." See how many times you can toss the potato back and forth before one of you misses. (Yep, you picked up the innuendo—*you* might be the one to miss!)
- Play Hopscotch. Decide on a table, such as the 7's or 8's, to practice. Players play in the usual way, but as they hop on each square, they must say the product of the square's number times the number of the chosen table.

- Play Multiplication War. Take the face cards out of a deck of cards and play the classic card game of War. In the Multiplication War version, however, as soon as players turn over their cards, they name the product of the cards. The player who gives the correct product first takes the cards.

➤ If your child is being taught to multiply larger numbers before he has had a chance to master the basic facts, *have him make a multiplication table* (see page 138) and work on the facts with him at another time. His inability to recall facts must not distract him from the important business of understanding the new concepts. If you suspect that your child is using the table as a crutch, keep it slightly out of reach. That way, he will have to make the effort to "look up" the fact just as he would look up a word's spelling in the dictionary.

➤ Practice multiplication facts with a twist. For example:
- What's the number of legs on two elephants times the number of legs on four ostriches?
- What's the number of letters in your first name times the number of letters in your last name?
- What's the number of days in a year times the number of feet on a fish?

➤ Slip multiplication problems into your everyday conversation. For example:
- You slept nine hours last night. Wow, how many minutes is that?
- They say one year in a dog's life is equal to seven human years. How old is Fido in human years?
- Well, let's see, your allowance is two dollars a week. How long is it going to take you to save up for that Nintendo game?

➤ In the car, "toss out" three numbers for your child to multiply. By tossing three rather than two numbers, you will be giving your child practice in multiplication facts as well as in mental computation skills. For example, if you toss out 5, 9, and 2, your child might notice that it is easier to multiply 5×2 first and then 10×9 to reach 90. Voilà! The commutative property of multiplication!

MULTIPLICATION ERRORS?

It is not unusual for numbers in multiplication problems to experience something akin to a continental shift. As a result, even a child with excellent multiplication skills can end up with a disheartening number of wrong answers. Suggest that your child do his computation work on graph paper—one number per square—or that he turn his papers sideways so that the lines make vertical columns for lining up the ones, tens, and hundreds.

➤ What's your child's age in years? In months? In days? In hours?

HAVE MORE TIME?

➤ Cut index cards into triangles and help your child make a set of fact triangles for the facts that are still causing him trouble. Unlike regular flash cards, fact triangles can represent all four related facts for any three given numbers. For example: $8 \times 7 = 56$; $7 \times 8 = 56$; $56 \div 7 = 8$; and $56 \div 8 = 7$. By placing your thumb over the corner showing the product, you can use these triangles as you would flash cards in games such as Multiplication Bingo (see below).

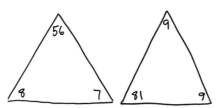

DOES YOUR CHILD REQUIRE MORE CONCRETE EXAMPLES OF MULTIPLICATION?

Show your child how to make an array lattice. At some point, your child has probably learned to use arrays—arrangements of objects in rows—to study multiplication. For example, $3 \times 4 = 12$ would look like this:

A slightly more abstract but still very visual way to show an array is to make a lattice and count the intersecting points. For example, for the problem 6×4, you would draw six horizontal lines and four intersecting vertical lines. The number of intersection points is the product of 6×4.

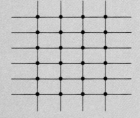

Or use place value blocks (see page 149) to show your child why the multiplication algorithm he is learning works. For example, for the problem 17 × 3 suggest that your child first make 17 with the blocks (one long and seven units). Have him repeat the procedure two more times for three groups of 17. Help him count the total number of blocks, exchanging ten units for one long whenever necessary. He should end up with five longs and one unit, or 51.

➤Play Multiplication Piggy. With two dice or number cubes you can also play the game of Multiplication Piggy—anytime, anywhere. The object of the game is to roll the dice and multiply the numbers so as to get as close to a score of 1,000 as possible. Here are the rules:

MULTIPLICATION PIGGY

1. Players take turns rolling the dice, multiplying sums in a cumulative manner. For example, a player might roll a 6 and a 2 to get 8, then roll a 3 and a 4 for 7. At this point, the player's score is 56 (8 × 7).
2. A player's turn continues until one of two things happens:
   • The player decides to end the turn, keeping the last product (84, in the example above) as his score.
   • The player rolls doubles. If a player rolls doubles, the turn automatically ends and the player's score for that turn goes down to 0.
3. The player whose score is closest to 1,000 after five rounds wins.

➤Play Multiplication Bingo. Here are the rules:

MULTIPLICATION BINGO

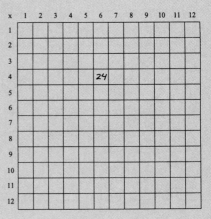

1. Make copies of the multiplication chart in the back of the book.
2. Use Triangle Fact Cards, flash cards, or a completed times table to choose and call out random multiplication facts, such as "Four times six!"
3. Each player writes the product of the fact in the proper place on the chart.
4. The first player to complete five products vertically, horizontally, or diagonally wins.

x	1	2	3	4	5	6	7	8	9	10	11	12
1												
2												
3												
4				24								
5												
6												
7												
8												
9												
10												
11												
12												

Division

The ability to divide whole numbers is measured by questions 1, 2, 6, and 7 on the Math Assessment.

Long division. The mere words turn even the most math-friendly heart to stone. Ask any adult to list his most dreaded math experiences and "long division" is bound to be near the top of the list. Why? The division we use each day comes as naturally as figuring out how many packages of hamburger buns we need (12 people ÷ 4 buns per package = 3 packages) or how many stickers each kid will get from a sheet of stickers (24 stickers ÷ 3 kids = 8). So why is long division so terrifying?

Because it is so darned complicated. Ask a fourth grader to divide a bag of 134 goldfish among her 23 classmates and she will carry off the task with aplomb, passing out certain numbers of goldfish until there are not enough left for the entire class. If nothing else, fourth graders are experts at fairness! But ask the same fourth grader to solve the problem 134 ÷ 23 and the results might be very different. Here are just a few of the difficulties she might encounter:

- Where do I put the numbers? Does the 134 come first (as in the equation) or does it go under the line?
- What do I do first, divide, multiply, or subtract?
- Where do I put the number?
- 23 doesn't go into 13, but I don't know my 23 tables. How do I know what number to choose?
- Where do I put the numbers?
- Oh-oh, 23 doesn't go into 134 evenly. What do I do with what's left?
- And where do I put the number?

If your child were to record what she did as she passed out goldfish, her solution might look like this:

$$
\begin{array}{r}
23\overline{)134} \\
-23 \quad 1 \\
\hline
111 \\
-23 \quad 1 \\
\hline
88 \\
-23 \quad 1 \\
\hline
65 \\
-23 \quad 1 \\
\hline
42 \\
-23 \quad 1 \\
\hline
19 \quad 5
\end{array}
$$

How many 23's?
5 with 19 left over.

If your child is a good estimator and is confident with her multiplication, she might not need as many steps to reach the answer:

$$23\overline{)134}$$
$$-92 \quad | \quad 4$$
$$\overline{42}$$
$$-23 \quad | \quad 1$$
$$\overline{19} \quad | \quad 5$$

How many 23's?
5 with 19 left over.

As she gains experience in estimating, she might even be able to move to the shorthand version of long division.

$$\begin{array}{r} 1 \quad\; 5 \; R\,19 \\ 23\overline{)134} \\ -115 \\ \hline 19 \end{array}$$

DIVISION ERRORS?

Let your child use graph paper for working out division problems. Long division only works if the numbers are properly aligned. *Do not underestimate how difficult this visual task is for most fourth graders.* If you don't have graph paper, suggest that your child turn her paper sideways and use the vertical lines as column guides.

Division is hard, but there are four simple ways that you can help make it easier.

1. Try not to pass along your own anxiety. Although it might be tempting to commiserate with your miserable fourth grader—"Eew! I *hated* long division when I was in fourth grade!"—such a response only serves as proof to your child that life's a drag. If to this day you still don't understand long division, ask your child to teach you. You will be modeling perseverance and the ability to take risks, and who knows, you might learn something. At the very least, it will be good for a few laughs.
2. Make sure your child has a solid understanding of place value, multiplication and its relationship to division, and subtraction. (See Understanding Place Value, page 143, and Multiplication, page 151.)
3. Help your child memorize her times tables, so that the facts are there when she needs them.
4. Find out which division procedure your child is learning in school and continually reinforce the sequence of steps at home.

Division is part of fourth grade. As the old chant says, "You can't go over it, you can't go under it, you can't go around it, you've got to go *through* it." With patience and lots of good humor, you and your child will both get through it.

> ## HELP YOUR CHILD REMEMBER THE STEPS FOR DIVIDING
>
> Chant the division steps—"Divide, Multiply, Subtract, and Bring Down"—over and over and over again. Suggest a mnemonic device to help your child remember the steps. One favorite is Does McDonald's Sell Burgers (Divide, Multiply, Subtract, and Bring Down), but your child might want to make up one of her own. If your child is musically inclined (or even if she isn't), suggest that she make up a jingle or rap for division steps:
>
> Yankee Doodle went to town,
> and said, "Divide, multiply, subtract, and bring *down!*"

HAVE FIVE MINUTES?

➤ Point out division situations in everyday life and ask "How can we find out?"
  - "I've only got a dollar. Is that enough for a week's worth of milk at school?"
  - "The computer is free for about forty-five minutes. How much time should each of you have on it?"
  - "We're driving at about fifty-five miles per hour. How long is it going to take us to get to Uncle Charlie's house?"

➤ Show your child how to estimate quotients. For example, if your child is faced with the problem $478 \div 6$, suggest that rounding might help her figure out what the answer might be. Point out that 478 is close to 480, which is easy to divide by 6. At other times, rounding both the divisor and the quotient might help. Rounding $1,898 \div 47$ into $2,000 \div 50$, for example, will at least give your child a ballpark starting point for division.

➤ Many fourth graders have a hard time with the idea of remainders. To encourage your child to think flexibly about remainders, talk about how remainders are used (or not used) in different situations. For example, ask your child how she would handle the remainder in the problem $11 \div 2$ in situations like these:
  - She is sharing eleven trading cards with her brother.
  - She is sharing eleven cups of water with her brother.
  - She is trying to figure out how many two-egg omelets she can make with eleven eggs.
  - She is sharing $11.00 with her brother.

➤In the grocery store, ask your child to help you figure out unit prices to compare different brands or sizes.

➤Need to keep a couple of fourth grade hands busy? Encourage your child to make a 0 to 99 like the one shown.

0	1	2	3	4	5	6	7	8	9
10	11	12	13	14	15	16	17	18	19
20	21	22	23	24	25	26	27	28	29
30	31	32	33	34	35	36	37	38	39
40	41	42	43	44	45	46	47	48	49
50	51	52	53	54	55	56	57	58	59
60	61	62	63	64	65	66	67	68	69
70	71	72	73	74	75	76	77	78	79
80	81	82	83	84	85	86	87	88	89
90	91	92	93	94	95	96	97	98	99

Have her use different colored pencils to cross out the following:
• Numbers divisible by 2.
• Numbers divisible by 3.
• Numbers divisible by 4.

Challenge your child to come up with divisibility rules for 2, 3, and 4 based on the patterns she sees in the chart. If your child likes this activity, follow the same procedure for numbers divisible by 5, 9, or 10. If your child is stumped, give her these rules to check on her chart.
• A number is divisible by 2 if it is an even number.
• A number is divisible by 3 if the sum of the digits is 3, 6, or 9.
• A number is divisible by 4 if the last two digits are divisible by 4.
• A number is divisible by 5 if it ends in 5 or 0.
• A number is divisible by 9 if the sum of its digits is divisible by 9.
• A number is divisible by 10 if it ends in 0.

HAVE MORE TIME?

➤To practice division facts, multiples, and factors (all of which help your child figure out the "goes into"—better known as the "gazinta"—stage of division), draw a cross pattern like the ones shown below. Ask your child which number in the pattern *doesn't* belong.

$$\frac{7 \quad | \quad 8}{9 \quad | \quad 63} \qquad \frac{64 \quad | \quad 16}{8 \quad | \quad 12} \qquad \frac{29 \quad | \quad 21}{35 \quad | \quad 28}$$

➤Play High Divide. All you need is a pencil, paper, and one die.

HIGH DIVIDE

1. Draw the following division form for each player.

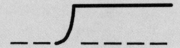

2. Take turns rolling the die and writing the number shown on one of the blanks in the division form. Continue until each player has filled her form with numbers.
3. Each player solves her division problem. The highest quotient (answer) wins.

➤Play Remainders. All you need are pencils and scrap paper.

REMAINDERS

1. Each person chooses a number between 20 and 100 and makes that many dots on the paper.
2. To choose a divisor, both people hold out a certain number of fingers at the same time and add the two numbers together. (You can do this in the style of the hand game Rock, Paper, Scissors if you want.)
3. Each player draws loops around the dots to make sets of the given divisor. For example, if the divisor is 5, the players loop groups of five dots. The remainder is the number of dots left over after all dots have been looped into sets. The player with the smallest remainder wins.

➤ Play Card Sharp. You can use this game to give your child practice in either division facts or in dividing larger numbers.

CARD SHARP

1. Remove all face cards from a deck of cards. Aces will serve as ones.
2. Deal three (or, for a more difficult game, four) cards face up in the center of the table.
3. Each player uses any combination of the numbers to form a division problem. For example, suppose the cards dealt were 2, 5, and 9. One player might choose to form $25 \div 9$ (2 R 7). Another might form $95 \div 2$ (47 R 1). Still another might make $29 \div 5$ (5 R 4).
4. The player with the *lowest remainder* wins. You might wish to play several rounds and add each player's remainders together for the final score.
5. You can also use this game for simple multiplication facts practice. Deal two cards to each player. The player whose cards make the highest product wins.

Fractions

The ability to work with fractions is measured by questions 2, 8, 9, 13, and 14 on the Math Assessment.

It is a sad but almost universal truth that, for most children, enthusiasm for math begins to flag somewhere between fourth and sixth grade. Many parents, teachers, and children do not hesitate to pin the blame for this "math slump" on fractions. Even children who have managed to make their way through long division can find fractions strange and befuddling. Witness the old saw: "Mine is not to reason why, just invert and multiply!"

In many ways, however, fractions cause unnecessary anxiety. Watch your child over the course of a weekend. Does he triple the amount of cocoa he uses to make hot chocolate for himself and two friends? Does he tell you that he has to be at soccer practice at a quarter to six? Does he disagree with the critic's 3 ½-star rating of his favorite movie? Does he struggle to play the sixteenth notes in his new piano piece fast enough? Each of these actions proves that your child is comfortable and adept at using fractions in his daily life. It is only when they are taken out of the context of real life that fractions begin to get confusing.

In many ways, fourth grade is a make-it-or-break-it year for your child's work in fractions. In most math programs, this year marks the transition between the concrete "cut the circle into two pieces" experiences of the primary grades and the difficult computation that looms ahead in fifth and sixth grade. If your child has spent the past three years comparing pieces of pizza, he will probably have little difficulty deciding if $1/2$ and $4/8$ equal the same part of the pie. If your child has not had a chance to build this understanding, however, he will have little more than a bundle of tricks (in this case, "multiply the top and the bottom by 4") to rely on in making the decision. Unfortunately, as the fractions your child works with get more complex, the list of tricks he needs to remember gets longer and longer.

You can help your child gain the critical understanding he needs by reinforcing these fundamental concepts:

- Fractions often tell about a part of a whole ($1/2$ of an orange) or a set ($1/2$ of the marbles).
- Fractions, like whole numbers, can have many different names, for example, $1/3$ can also be called (or is *equivalent to*) $2/6$ or $3/9$ or $4/12$.
- Special words are used to describe fractions.

  Parts of a fraction: the *numerator* is the number of parts being considered; the denominator is the total number of parts.

  Proper fraction: a fraction that is less than a whole; with a proper fraction the denominator is greater than the numerator: $3/4$

  Improper fraction: a fraction that is equal to or more than one whole; with an improper fraction the numerator is greater than or equal to the denominator: $6/4$

  Mixed numeral: a whole number and a fraction: $1\,1/5$

Whenever possible, use concrete materials such as the fraction strips and the pattern blocks in the back of the book to help your child see how fractions work. Be sure to vary the materials so that your child doesn't always visualize $1/4$ as a quarter of a pizza or $1/8$ as an eighth of an inch. The more concrete, real-life experience you can give your child with fractions now, the smoother the fraction work ahead will be.

HAVE FIVE MINUTES?

➤ Enlist your child's services in the kitchen. Every half cup of water or two-eighths stick of butter he uses will give him a valuable lesson in fraction concepts. Ask your child to help you double or halve a recipe. Then encourage him to write a recipe of his own. Next, challenge him to rewrite the recipe so that it will serve twice as many people.

➤ Point out times when the fraction bar (the /, as in $1/2$) means "out of" and when it means "divided by." For example:

- You've already done 3 *out of* 4 of your math problems. That's ¾ of your assignment.
- There are 4 of us, but only 3 cupcakes—3 *divided by* 4 is ¾. We each can have ¾ of a cupcake.

➤Make number soup. On a magnetic board or piece of paper taped to the refrigerator, draw a large circle. Inside the circle, draw or write a fraction, as shown below. See how many different names for that fraction your family can come up with during the course of the day.

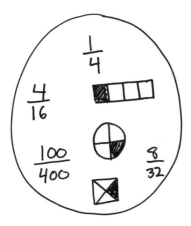

➤Point out and talk about the fraction marks on rulers. Ask your child to hypothesize why some marks on the ruler are missing, such as the ⅜, ¼, ⁴⁄₈, and ⁶⁄₈ on the ruler below. To help your child with the equivalents, have him fold a strip of paper in half, quarters, and eighths, marking the fold(s) with the proper fraction each time.

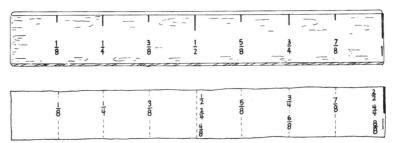

HAVE MORE TIME?

➤Trace or make at least two copies of the fraction strips patterns on page 218 and have your child cut them out. Use the strips for activities such as these:

- Mix up the pieces. Ask your child to use the strips to make "trains" that are equal in length, as shown. After he has created a number of trains, help him record the equivalents in fraction notation.

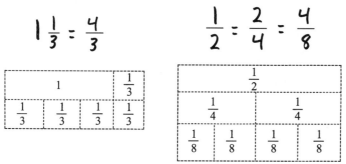

- Challenge your child to find different ways to cover a 1 (one whole) strip.

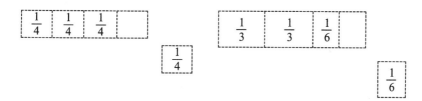

- Ask your child to use the fraction strips to make up addition and subtraction problems. For example: ⅕ + ⅕ + ⅕ = ⅗.

➤Make pattern block designs with your child. If you can, invest in a set of pattern blocks. Sets of plastic or wooden pattern blocks are available in most toy stores and catalogs. You can also use the patterns at the back of the book to make your own set out of poster board. You will need at least ten of each shape (twenty-five is even better). Each shape should be a different color so that you can talk about the blocks by color. Chances are, you will be amazed at the elaborate designs your child is able to make with these blocks. As he explores, you can ask questions such as
  - Which block is half the size of the blue diamond?
  - How many reds will cover one yellow block? So one red covers how much of the yellow?
  - Can you make a design that is half blue and half red?

➤Play Fraction Roll. Take turns rolling two dice or number cubes. Use the numbers shown to make a *proper* fraction. For example, if you roll a 5 and a 2, you can make ⅖. Use the fraction strips to compare the fractions. The player with the larger fraction wins. Include improper fractions *only after* your child is very comfortable with proper fractions and has been introduced to improper fractions.

➤ Play with paper or napkin folding. Ask "If you fold the paper in half, how many sections will you have? How about if you fold it in half again?" Have your child fold and refold the paper to check his predictions.

➤ Play Fraction Pickup. Here are the simple rules:

FRACTION PICKUP

1. Place the fraction strips from page 219 in a paper bag.
2. Each player draws a strip from the bag and the players compare their strips.
3. Each player makes a fist, and on the count of three holds out one or two fingers (Rock, Paper, Scissors style). If the total number of fingers is even, the player with the largest fraction gets one tally mark. If the total is odd, the player with the smallest fraction gets the mark.
4. The first player to get 5 tally marks wins.

Decimals

The ability to work with decimals is measured by questions 2, 3, and 13 on the Math Assessment.

Adults deal with decimals every day—in the grocery store, at the gas pump, on their car's odometer, and in the sports pages of the newspaper. On calculators and electronic scales decimal notation (2.25 lbs.) replaces fraction notation (2¼ lbs.) in everyday figuring. And at least once in their lives, most adults have experienced the terror of a misplaced decimal point—"I owe *what*?" Children, too, deal with decimals when they handle money, check their favorite players' batting averages, or have their temperature taken.

Unless they are rooted in real-life experience, decimals can seem overcomplicated and unfathomable to a young person's eye. Think of the child who punches 1 ÷ 3 into a calculator and comes up with 0.33333333. Whoa! Where did *that* come from? In fourth grade, what your child already knows about decimals will begin to be formalized into lessons on decimal notation and calculation. Your job this year is to help demystify decimals by reinforcing these simple concepts:

- A decimal is another name for a fraction.
- The decimal place value system is based on ten, just like the whole number system, so that .1 equals 1/10, .01 equals 1/100, and so on.

- Decimals are read as tenths, hundredths, thousandths, and so on. The decimal point is read as "and." For example: 1.9 = one *and* nine-tenths; 48.29 = forty-eight *and* twenty-nine hundredths.
- Adding and subtracting decimals is just like adding and subtracting whole numbers, as long as you keep the numbers and decimal points aligned.

HAVE FIVE MINUTES?

➤ Notice, read aloud, and talk about decimals that you come across in the course of your day. In the grocery store, have your child read aloud the weight showing on the electronic scale. Ask "Is that closer to two pounds or three pounds?"

➤ Send your child on a decimal scavenger hunt. Where can she find them? On food packages? In the newspaper? In the *Guinness Book of Records*? Challenge her to look for and write down the decimal numbers she can find. Invite her to pick her favorite recorded decimal, read it aloud, and tell you what the decimal means. For example: "The Olympic skier won by one-hundredth of a second!"

➤ In the car, challenge your child with brainteasers such as:
  - What's the smallest number less than 1 that you can make using the numbers 2, 4, and 6?
  - Which would you rather have, .2 of a dollar or .19 of a dollar?
  - What's the next number in this sequence: .1, .15, .2, __

➤ Propose that your child keep track of the number of miles you drive taking her to school, lessons, friends' houses, and so on, for one week. Keep a small notebook in the car and show her how to use the car's trip odometer to record the mileage. If your car doesn't have a trip odometer, have her record the mileage at the beginning and end of each journey. At the end of the week, use a calculator to add up the final mileage. Perhaps you should start charging 10¢ per mile!

➤ Making change is excellent practice in decimal computation. Make sure your child knows how to "count up" from the cost, starting with the smallest coins first. Whenever possible, let your child pay for purchases herself and count her change. If you give your child an allowance or pay for her odd jobs, give her the money in large bills or coins and ask her to make change for you.

➤ Do you spend more money on junk food or vegetables? After a shopping trip, have your child make a chart. As you put away the groceries, call out the cost of each item. (For scanned items, have your child find the cost on the sales receipt.) After your child records each item's price on the chart, help her add up the totals in the columns. (For large shopping trips, use a calculator.) Now you know where all the money goes!

➤In decimal computation, as in multiplication and long division, neatness counts. Help your child keep her decimals from going astray by using graph paper or setting up grids such as these.

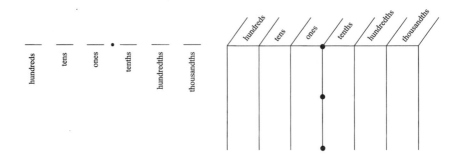

HAVE MORE TIME?

➤Make copies of the centimeter squares in the back of the book (see page 218). Cut out a large square of 10 × 10 blocks. Ask your child to tell you how many squares are in the large square (100). Then ask her to color in ten of the squares. Ask "What part of the whole did you color?" (.1 or .10) Next, suggest that your child color in any number of squares. Again ask what part is colored. When you are sure that your child understands that each square is one hundredth of the whole, encourage her to make her own design on a fresh 10 × 10 square and ask again "What part of the whole have you colored?"

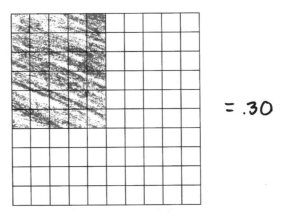

= .30

➤Play Roll a Decimal. Here's how:

ROLL A DECIMAL

1. Use one die or a deck of cards. If using cards, remove the tens and face cards from the deck.
2. Each player draws the following grid on a sheet of paper:

———— • ———— ————

3. Players take turns rolling the die or choosing a card and writing the number shown in any available space on their grid.
4. After all the spaces are filled, players read their numbers aloud. The player with the largest number wins.

➤Play Where's the Point? Make up statements like the ones below and ask your child to tell you where the decimal point should go to make them correct.
- A gallon of milk costs $225.
- A good racer can run 225 miles per hour.
- A football player weighs about 225 pounds.

➤To practice computation with money, play Money Muffins. Set a muffin tin or a number of small bowls on the floor. Grab a handful of change from your pocket or the family change jar and place a few coins in each cup or bowl. Players take turns tossing beanbags or stones into the cups and adding together (or, for a more difficult game, multiplying) the totals of their throws. The first person to reach $5.00 is the winner. To practice subtraction, players start with $5.00 and subtract their throws until one player reaches zero.

Geometry

Your child's understanding of geometry is assessed by questions 10 and 11 on the Math Assessment.

Until recently, children studied geometry when they learned their shapes in kindergarten and then again in high school geometry class. In the years between, they learned arithmetic. Most elementary math textbooks gave geometry a light once-over in the back of the book, with the implicit suggestion that it was to be studied only after the "real" work of computation had been completed.

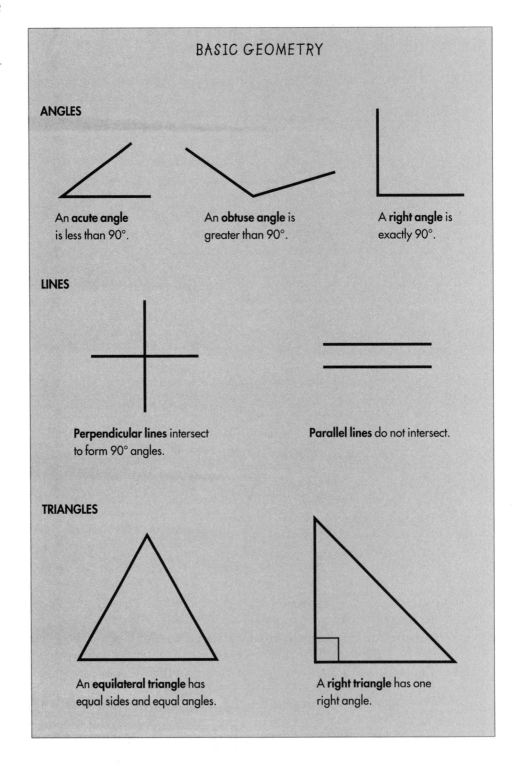

BASIC GEOMETRY

ANGLES

An **acute angle** is less than 90°.

An **obtuse angle** is greater than 90°.

A **right angle** is exactly 90°.

LINES

Perpendicular lines intersect to form 90° angles.

Parallel lines do not intersect.

TRIANGLES

An **equilateral triangle** has equal sides and equal angles.

A **right triangle** has one right angle.

BASIC GEOMETRY

QUADRILATERALS

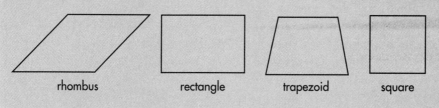

rhombus   rectangle   trapezoid   square

The square, rectangle, and rhombus are also called **parallelograms** because they have two sets of parallel sides.

SOLIDS

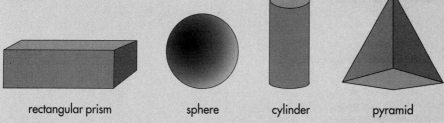

rectangular prism   sphere   cylinder   pyramid

FORMULAS

Area is computed by multiplying a plane figure's length times its width.
Perimeter is the distance around a plane figure.
Volume is the number of cubic units in a solid.

CIRCLE

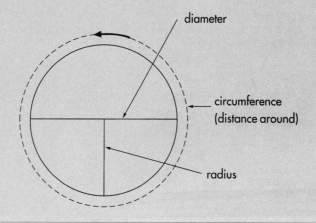

diameter

circumference
(distance around)

radius

Times have changed. Today, more and more educators are emphasizing that mathematics is more than just arithmetic. The math you use every time you read a map or put away the dishes or buy new wallpaper or park your car is geometry, not arithmetic. Strong math programs develop children's intuitive understanding of geometry by providing lots of concrete opportunities to create and manipulate shapes of all sorts. If you are lucky, your fourth grader will continue to develop spatial thinking skills in much the same way.

In many schools, however, the study of geometry takes on a different look in the fourth grade year. Children who in the past had great fun drawing and folding and constructing shapes now sit grim-faced in front of workbook sheets filled with definitions and formulas. No wonder so many fourth graders seem to lose their delight in mathematics!

Luckily, no matter how drearily geometry is taught at school, it can still be fun at home. Simple pastimes like working jigsaw puzzles or building a birdhouse will reinforce your child's understanding of geometric principles such as area and perimeter and strengthen his ability to think spatially.

HAVE FIVE MINUTES?

➤ Speak the language of geometry. Point out geometric figures and their attributes, and call each by name. Don't worry if you don't know a rhombus from a trapezoid. Take a guess, ask your child's opinion, and then check your guesses at a convenient time. You might find that what you call a rhombus, your child calls a parallelogram—and that you're both correct! For easy reference, a list of geometric terms generally taught in fourth grade follows this section.

➤ Got a fourth grader hanging around the kitchen? Invite him to test his visual memory. Open the refrigerator or a cupboard and give your child about five seconds to gaze at the contents. Send him out of the room and take one item out of the refrigerator. When your child returns, see if he can guess the missing item.

The more you stretch your child's visual memory, the more you are helping him in his study of geometry. For another visual memory activity, challenge your child to draw an item—a paper clip, a pencil, or his foot, for example—from memory, matching both the shape *and size* of the item. Compare his drawings with the actual items. Which drawing came closest to the real thing?

➤ If your child is struggling to memorize geometrical terms, liven things up by drawing a rhombus, parallel lines, and so on with your finger on her back. Or invite your child to use toothpicks or straws to create each figure you name. Whenever you have a few extra minutes and a pen and paper, draw four figures. Ask "Which of these doesn't belong?"

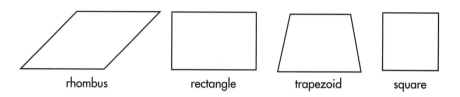

rhombus   rectangle   trapezoid   square

➤ If your child doesn't know how to use a coordinate grid to locate places on a map, now is the time to teach him. Then use city maps, subway maps, state maps, even the map at the mall, to test your child's navigation skills. It might take you a bit longer to get where you're going, but your child's increased spatial awareness and practice in coordinate geometry will be worth the trouble.

➤ Draw your child's initials in geometric shapes on the back of a place mat or napkin. Have your child place a knife perpendicular to the shape to see its mirrored reflection. Invite him to draw the shape he sees on the opposite side of the knife. The resulting shape should be symmetrical.

➤ If you are traveling, keep a handful of toothpicks in your purse or pocket. Keep your child occupied by presenting challenges such as:
  • How many letters can you make?
  • How many enclosed shapes can you make?
  • How many shapes can you make with five toothpicks?
  • Can you move four toothpicks so that there are only four triangles in the diagram below? (For the solution to this one, check page 177.)

➤ If you can't wade through the mess in your child's room, try a new approach. Ask him to estimate how many rectangles need putting away. (Did you know that the flattened top of a dirty sock makes a rectangle? How many spheres are under that bed?) For added incentive, have him tally the shapes he finds and pay him a penny a shape.

HAVE MORE TIME?

➤ Make or buy a geoboard. Inexpensive commercial geoboards are available on the market, but your child will have a much better time making one himself by hammering sixteen nails into a block of wood as shown. Making designs on geoboards is a great way to reinforce all sorts of geometrical concepts. Here are just a few.

- Attributes and terminology: "How many different kinds of triangles can you make?"
- Perimeter: "Can you make a shape that touches three pegs? How about four? How about five?"
- Area: "How many little squares would fit inside that big shape you just made?"
- Congruence: "Can you make a shape that is exactly like the one I made?"
- Symmetry: "Let's see if we can make a symmetrical design by taking turns putting on different rubber bands."

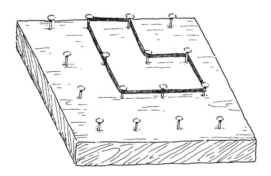

➤ On a hike or walk through the park, encourage your child to look carefully for examples of geometrical elements occurring in nature.

- pentagons, hexagons, and other polygons
- symmetry
- spirals
- right, obtuse, and acute angles
- parallel and perpendicular lines

➤ Invite your fourth grader to create a coat of arms for your family. Tell him that he can use any shapes or symbols he wants to represent the family *as long as the design is symmetrical.* If you have a home computer, your child might enjoy using its graphics program to complete the design work.

➤ If your child is confused about angle measurements he is not alone. Many optical illusions are based on the awareness that people see angles differently the nearer or farther they are from an angle. You might try talking about angles in terms of the clock (3:00 is a right angle) or by having your child show you various angles with his arms.

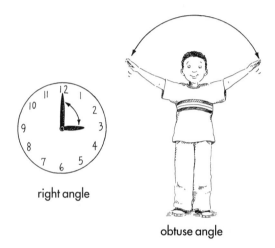

right angle

obtuse angle

➤ Ask your child to help you cut a variety of shapes from cardboard: different kinds and sizes of triangles, rectangles, trapezoids, polygons (such as hexagons and octagons), and circles. Then suggest that your child sort the shapes. Why did he sort the shapes the way he did? What is the same or different about the shapes in each group?

➤ If your child is having a hard time remembering a geometrical term or concept, such as *congruent* or *parallel lines,* suggest that she make a book that explains the term to younger kids. If you don't have a younger child in your house, arrange to give the book to a younger class at your child's school. (Don't worry, the effort will be met with grace, if not gratitude!)

➤ Play games with coordinates. Most fourth graders have played a version of Battleship, in which they try to "sink" another player's ship by guessing its position on a grid. You can make your own game geared toward your child's individual interests. First, decide on a theme. Collecting rare gems? Rounding up wild ponies? Make two copies of the centimeter square paper in the back of the book (see page 216) and mark each grid with coordinates as shown. Each player secretly marks an *X* on his grid for each item (gem, horse, etc.) to be found. Players take turns trying to find each other's *X*'s by naming pairs of coordinates. The first player to discover all the other's *X*'s wins.

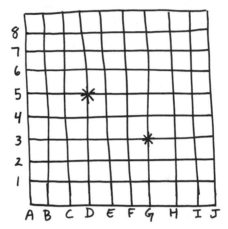

The rare gems are at (D5) and (G3)

➤ Have fun with tessellations. Tesselating shapes fit together in infinite patterns without any gaps or overlaps. Go to the library and check out books or prints of M. C. Escher's famous tessellations. The idea that some shapes fit together to form such elaborate patterns is fascinating to fourth graders. Invite your child to use the pattern pieces in the back of the book to make tessellating patterns of his own.

If you can find it (try educational toy stores and catalogs), the game Tessera makes an excellent gift for this age group. Watch out—you might not be able to keep your hands off those tessellating beetles yourself!

➤ Suggest that your child take up origami or paper airplane folding. Most fourth graders have the dexterity to create fairly elaborate creations with folded paper. Books of origami and paper airplane designs are available at bookstores and in your library. Once your child is familiar with some of the basic paper-folding principles, encourage him to create master-pieces of his own design as well.

Solution to toothpick puzzle, page 173.

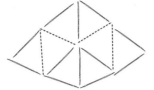 

Remove the toothpicks shown by dotted lines.

Measurement

The ability to use measurement to solve problems is assessed by questions 11 and 12 on the Math Assessment.

Ah, measurement. If you have been sweating over long division or struggling to remember how to compare fractions with different denominators, you might turn to this section with a sigh of relief. Finally, here's something both you and your child can get your hands on. No more petulant arguments that begin "Why am I gonna have to know this stuff?" Even the most math-resistant fourth grader has had moments when being able to measure things has come in handy. And surely your child knows most of this "stuff" by now anyway. What could be more basic than knowing how to measure?

By fourth grade your child has a lot of measurement experience behind her. She knows how to use a ruler, whether liquids are measured in inches or cups, and if she needs to wear a jacket when the thermometer reads 32°F. If she does a lot of carpentry or cooking with you, she might even know that there are thirty-six inches in a yard or eight ounces in a cup. It seems only fair that in this area at least she should be able to relax a bit and rest on her laurels.

There is, however, no rest for the weary. This year, your child will be facing brave new worlds in measurement. She will be exploring both customary and metric units of measure for length, capacity, weight, mass, and temperature, and working with fractional

TOOLS OF THE TRADE

Be sure that you have proper measurement tools around the house. Place an analog clock and a calendar in clear view and refer to them often. Have a ruler and measuring cup available for easy reference. Other tools that might come in handy are

- yardstick
- meter stick
- tape measure
- measuring spoons
- bathroom scale
- balance scale with metric weights
- thermometer with both Fahrenheit and Celsius scales

parts of each. If she hasn't done so before, she will learn how to figure elapsed time and how to measure the area, perimeter, and volume of geometric figures. In a strong math program, your child will continue to learn about measurement through hands-on experience in estimating, measuring, and comparing measures. This is especially important with new concepts such as area or volume. If your child is coming home with worksheets of formulas or conversion tables, it is doubly important that you give her as much concrete experience as possible at home. Real-life measuring activities will give your child experience with number sense, estimation, computation, and problem solving as well as practice in using different units of measure.

Measurement activities are also included in the Number Sense (page 135), Estimating (page 140), and Geometry (page 169) sections of this book.

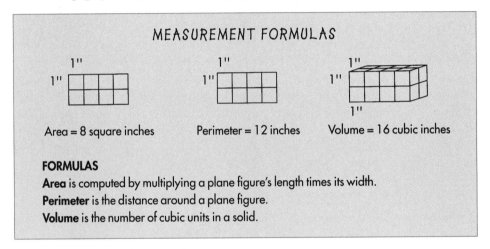

MEASUREMENT FORMULAS

Area = 8 square inches   Perimeter = 12 inches   Volume = 16 cubic inches

FORMULAS
Area is computed by multiplying a plane figure's length times its width.
Perimeter is the distance around a plane figure.
Volume is the number of cubic units in a solid.

HAVE FIVE MINUTES?

➤ Estimate everything. Then measure.
- How wide was that puddle your child just jumped?
- How far is it to the nearest bus stop?
- How long can your child hold her breath?
- Which backpack has the greatest capacity?

If you don't have a standard measuring tool handy, use your child's personal references (see the activity below) or one of the following rules of thumb:
- 1 inch = a thumb's knuckle to its tip (ever wonder where the expression "rule of thumb" came from?)
- 1 centimeter = the width of a little finger
- 6 inches = the width of a hand with fingers spread out

- 1 foot = a man's foot, or the width of two hands with fingers spread out
- 1 decimeter = a woman's foot
- 1 yard or meter = a man's stride, or from fingertip to nose
- 1 cup = two hands cupped together
- 1 backpack = six missing pencils, one scrunched-up homework folder, two overdue library books, a permission slip for last week's field trip, one Nerf football, three beanbag animals, half a bag of stale popcorn . . .

➤ Encourage your child to come up with her own set of personal references for different units of measure. The standard measures we use today evolved from basic body measurements. A yard, for example, measured from the tip of the nose to the end of one's outstretched arm. Give your child a ruler and a measuring cup and see if she can come up with a set of references that she will have with her always (or at least until she grows).

➤ Take note of the units of measure used in every-day life. Distance on most U.S. highway signs is shown in miles, but sports events may be measured in meters or kilometers. Some products, such as soft drinks, are sold in metric sizes, while others, such as canned vegetables, are sold in U.S. customary measures.

> **IS YOUR CHILD MEASURING CORRECTLY?**
>
> If your child is still having difficulty using a ruler, it might be because she doesn't know where to start measuring. Many children reason that if you start counting with 1, you should start measuring with 1 (that is, at the 1 inch or 1 centimeter mark). Have your child stand with her heels against a wall and count the steps she takes as she walks forward. She will see that she starts counting at the first step, not at the wall. In the same way, she starts measuring at the end, or 0 mark on a ruler, not at the 1.

Most fourth grade math programs include lessons on both customary and metric measures (centimeters, grams, liters, and so on). Ask your child or her teacher which system she is currently studying at school. *Do not attempt to teach your child how to covert from one system to the other.* Instead, talk about benchmarks. It is much more useful for your fourth grader to know that the temperature on a nice day is about 72°F or about 22°C than to know the formula for converting the Fahrenheit scale to Celsius.

➤ Area and perimeter are difficult to understand because the units of measure used for each can change. A square-acre plot of land is not the same as a square mile of land. Nor does a 2-centimeter-by-3-centimeter rectangle have the same perimeter as a 2-inch-by-3-inch rectangle. Each might have a perimeter of 10, but ten *what*?

To understand the sense behind these measures, your child needs a lot of experience just playing around with the ideas of area and perimeter. Give her a pile of Scrabble tiles or playing cards and challenge her to create different shapes, such as:

- A shape that has an area of sixteen playing cards.
- As many shapes as she can that have a perimeter of eight tile edges.
- Two shapes, one of which has twice the area or perimeter of the other.

Try very hard not to teach your child formulas such as length × width = area or 2l + 2w = perimeter. If she comes up with these rules on her own, so much the better—she will probably remember them her whole life long. If not, you can be assured that she will eventually be drilled on these formulas at school. What you can provide at home that she might *not* get at school is the hands-on experimentation that builds meaning and understanding.

➤ Bring back that old time passer, I Spy. It's probably been a while since you last kept your child busy with "I spy with my little eye—" This tougher version will be a challenge for both of you. I spy with my little eye—

- something that is between six inches and a foot long.
- something that weighs about as much as you do.
- something that can hold about a half a cup of liquid.

➤ Do you ever feel that simply getting your child out the door in the morning is equal to a full day's work? Encourage your child to set her own schedule. How much time does she need to get dressed? Eat breakfast? Find her other sneaker? Have her write out a big, bold morning schedule and post it on the refrigerator. How is her actual schedule comparing? Does she need more time? What are some ways she can create more time, besides waking up earlier?

➤ "Are we there yet?" Fend off this inevitable traveling question by helping your child estimate the amount of time your trip will take. Note the starting time of your trip. Then, at various intervals, ask "How much time do you think has passed?" At each interval, award one point to the person whose estimate of the elapsed time was closest. The person with the most points when you reach your destination wins the challenge.

HAVE MORE TIME?

➤ Do a project together. Fourth grade is the height of project mania. In fact, your fourth grader probably already has a project or two up her sleeve. If she doesn't have one of her own, enlist her help in household projects such as painting the porch banisters or planting this year's garden. On a smaller scale, make an unbirthday cake or set up a weather station. Turn a pair of cutoff jeans into a backpack or a pile of sand and rocks into a mini-civilization. Create jewelry or model airplanes or stained-glass ornaments or homemade candles. Or choose a project from any of the many craft books and kits available in bookstores and the library. Most fourth graders have well-developed fine motor skills and a keen eye for detail. Take advantage of these strengths by encouraging projects that require exact measurements—and don't forget to pass along the old carpenter's adage: Measure twice, cut once.

➤ Experiment with circumference (the distance around a circle). How can your child measure the distance around her waist? How does that distance compare with the distance around her head?

➤ Make a tape measure. There is something about a tape measure that is highly appealing to a fourth grader. Your child can make a simple tape measure by cutting two long strips of masking tape and sticking the sticky sides together. Have her use a ruler to mark off inches, feet, and yards (or centimeters and meters, depending upon the system your child is currently studying at school), and mark each foot or decimeter in a different color to make the tape easier to read.

➤ Create a race course together. A race course can be as simple as a cardboard tube marble run or as elaborate as a slalom course for snowboarding. Help your child decide how to measure the distance of the course and to time the speed of the racers, and encourage her to keep records of the races for use in predicting winners (see Statistics and Probability, below).

Statistics and Probability

The ability to work with statistics and probability is measured by questions 13 and 14 on the Math Assessment.

"Now," sputtered the White Rabbit, "if a chance had a law, it wouldn't be a chance, and it'd have to go to jail for breaking the law, wouldn't it, perchance?"
　　　　　　　　　　—Lewis Carroll, *Alice's Adventures in Wonderland*

Open the newspaper and read the headlines. PRESIDENT'S APPROVAL RATING AT 42%. STOCK MARKET EXPECTED TO REACH NEW HIGHS IN TRADING. BUY NEW DOUBLE CHOCOLATE LITE WITH 1/3 THE FAT OF OTHER CHOCOLATES! Though statistics and probability influence how and where we live, how we vote, and what kind of food we buy, we find them slippery at best. If the statistics support our inclinations—STUDY SHOWS EATING CHOCOLATE REDUCES HEART DISEASE!—we love them. If they seem to bear bad tidings—INCREASE IN HEART ATTACKS LINKED TO CHOCOLATE!—we do our best to discredit or disregard them.

Most children adore statistics. They love discovering that the kids in their class have an average of 1.8 siblings, and giggle over which of their beloved brothers or sisters might account for the .8. They love world records and numerical twists of fate and the touch of wizardry that the laws of probability lend to "ordinary" mathematics. Statistics are all about information, and children sense from an early age that information is powerful. The task is to learn how to make sense of all that information. Children need to learn how information is collected, how it is organized and interpreted, and how any one of those factors might affect its validity.

Traditionally, probability and statistics were not taught until sixth grade or beyond. Today, it is not uncommon to see kindergartners making graphs of sunny and cloudy days and fifth graders using records from the *Old Farmer's Almanac* to predict the weather for next week's field day. This year your fourth grader will continue to collect data and organize it into graphs, perform simple probability experiments, and probably learn how to find an average for a set of data. By providing experiences in collecting information and predicting outcomes at home, you can help your child become more comfortable with the concepts of probability and data analysis both at school and in the world around him.

HAVE FIVE MINUTES?

➤ Speak the language of chance. Most fourth graders' vocabularies already contain expressions of probability: *sure, 50-50 chance, impossible, no way,* and the perennial favorite, *yeah, right!* Other terms, such as *forecast* or *probability,* might not be as familiar. Talk about what is certain (besides death and taxes) and what is not, what is likely to occur, and what is close to impossible. Point out that many of the decisions your child makes each day ("Should I wear pants or shorts today?") are affected by the likelihood that something will or will not happen.

➤ Point out statistics wherever you can find them, and talk about how they are calculated. If your child is a baseball fanatic, but you don't know the difference between an RBI and an ERA, have *him* explain the statistics to you. Don't hesitate to wrestle with the numbers. You could do a lot worse than to instill in your child a healthy skepticism about "how they got" any given statistics.

➤ How long did it take your child to get dressed this morning? Yesterday morning? How about the day before? Suggest that she keep track of the number of minutes it takes her to get dressed each day, then find the average. Does her schedule give her enough time in the morning?

Monday	Tuesday	Wednesday	Thursday	Friday
20	15	24	20	17

$$\text{Average} = \frac{20 + 15 + 24 + 20 + 17}{5} = 19.2 \text{ minutes per day}$$

➤ Send your child on a graph scavenger hunt. How many different kinds of graphs can he find in the daily newspaper? What kind of information does each one give? Are they labeled clearly? Do they have any missing information? Who collected the information? Is there another way the same information could be shown? Which way is better?

➤ Graph your habits. Post a bar graph outline on the refrigerator. Ask family members to make an X in the appropriate column each time they open the refrigerator. At the end of a week, compare your findings. Other family habits to graph include:
   • time spent reading, watching television, or sleeping
   • chores completed
   • math facts memorized
   • times teeth are brushed
   • telephone calls answered

Number of Times Refrigerator Was Opened

			X
			X
X			X
X	X		X
X	X	X	X
X	X	X	X
MOM	DAD	SIS	BRO

➤ Talk about the meaning of the percent sign (%). Percentages go hand in hand with fractions and decimals (25% = 25/100 = .25), yet most math programs do not formally introduce the concept until fifth or sixth grade. Many children already know about percentages from following sports statistics. If your child doesn't, simply explain that the % sign means "out of one hundred." Does that make his 50% chance of having pizza for dinner sound better or worse?

HAVE MORE TIME?

➤ Play a game of probability with dice or number cubes. Throw a pair of dice and keep track of the number of times each number comes up. Which number occurs most frequently? Talk about your predictions and why certain numbers might come up more frequently than others.

➤ The next time you get out the Monopoly or any other game board, challenge your child to figure out which spaces are landed on most often. Is it better to buy Boardwalk or Illinois Avenue? St. James Place or Reading Railroad? The results might just change your playing strategies!

➤ Read *In the Next Three Seconds*, by Rowland Morgan (Lodestar). This fun book is filled with amazing predictions (watch your watch; in the next three days alone, $11 million worth of jewelry will be stolen from Americans) and backs them with statistics and an explanation of how the predictions are made.

➤ Most fourth graders love collecting information, especially about themselves and their friends. Encourage your budding pollster to make a list of intriguing questions. (You might have to make sure the questions aren't *too* intriguing!) Help your child decide on the best way to organize and publish his results.

➤ Pass the time on a dreary Saturday or a long car ride by performing probability experiments. Invite your child to predict the outcome of the experiment first, and then check the results of the experiment against the prediction. Eventually, your child should come to the conclusion that the more often he repeats an experiment, the more reliable his predictions will be. You can find probability experiments in any book of math activities, or suggest one of the easy experiments below.
  • Draw a 10 × 10 square chart. Have your child color the following squares: 1 red, 4 blue, 10 yellow, 10 green, 25 black, 50 white. Toss a coin or marker onto the chart 100 times. What are the chances of the coin's hitting a square of each color?

- Make a spinner as shown in the For Kids Only booklet. Have your child color different parts of the circle different colors. How does the size of each part affect the likelihood of the spinner's landing on that color?
- Toss a die or flip a coin. How does the likelihood that a certain outcome (for example, heads or the number 6) will come up change with the number of tosses?
- Place Scrabble or Boggle tiles in a bag and draw one letter at a time. Which letter do you think will be drawn most often? Why?

➤Many word processing programs have graph-making capabilities. If you have access to such a program, use it to show your child how the same information can be organized into different kinds of graphs. Knowing how to handle these tools will be a useful skill throughout your child's academic career.

➤Teach your child poker. (You might also remind him that the odds against getting a royal flush are 649,739 to 1.)

➤Play around with combinations. Suppose your child has nothing but three odd socks in his drawer. Rather than rush down to the washing machine, encourage him to think of all the combinations he could make with just those three socks. Suggest that your child draw pictures or make a systematic list to figure out the many options open to him.

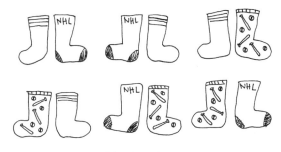

W = plain white
NHL = hockey
BB = baseball

Left Foot	Right Foot
W	NHL
NHL	W
W	BB
BB	W
NHL	BB
BB	NHL

Math Enrichment

It happens when you're least expecting it. You're searching your wallet for your child's library card, and she calmly tells you, "My number is 5124618." You're trying to explain how "they" want her to write out the steps on a workbook page of long division and she exclaims in frustration, "But why can't I just put down 134 and 3/29?" You look at your child with a mixture of pride and apprehension. What's going on here?

Some children seem to have a knack for math. For these children, mathematics just makes sense—it seems like a great way to organize the world. If your child is watching *Wall Street Week* and converting dollars to yen on the weekend, you might question the sheets of multiplication problems she is bringing home during the week. Shouldn't somebody be challenging her to bigger and better things? And if it isn't her teachers, shouldn't that somebody be you?

The answer is yes—and no. Yes, by all means challenge her at home. Ask her to figure out how much she will spend on hot lunches at school this year, or how the odds were figured for the National League playoffs. But challenging does not necessarily mean jumping ahead. The fact that your child can polish off a sheet of long division problems with ease does not mean that you should give her a sheet full of fractions to divide. A worksheet of fractions is not a reward, it's a punishment. Instead, cater to her natural delight in the way numbers work by providing her with puzzles, games, and real-life dilemmas that stretch her problem-solving and mathematical reasoning skills.

Your child might be hiding the proof of Fermat's last theorem behind her Goosebumps book, or she might just be ready for an extra mathematical charge. Either way, her enthusiasm for math, her confidence in her own mathematical abilities, and her ease in approaching new problems all depend greatly on your ability to keep math an active, interesting part of both your lives. Don't be afraid to say "I don't know—let's see if we can find out" and learn together. Who knows, it might be fun.

HAVE FIVE MINUTES?

➤ Invent Magic Squares. Your child probably met her first magic square in first grade. However, magic squares come in all shapes and sizes. If your sophisticated fourth grader complains that magic squares are for babies, challenge her with one of these. Then dare her to invent a magic square that will stump you! (For the faint of heart, solutions can be found on page 191.)

1. Use the numerals 1 through 12. Each row or column of 4 boxes should equal 22.

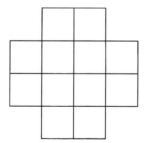

2. Use the numerals 1 through 9. Each side should equal 21.

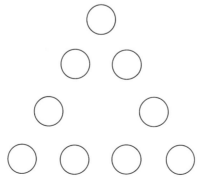

3. Use the numerals 1 through 9. The sum of each row of circles should equal 15.

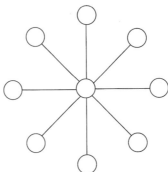

➤ Play Where Are We Now? Give your child an ongoing problem, such as "Start with 10, add 7, multiply by 2, subtract 4. Where are we now?" If you agree on where you should be (30), continue the problem. See how long you can keep the problem going before you come to a point where you disagree about "where are we now."

➤ Be on the lookout for faulty logic. Give your child practice by asking her to find the fault in the logic behind statements such as "There's a 50 percent chance of rain on Saturday and a 50 percent chance of rain on Sunday. Oh dear, that's a 100 percent chance of rain this weekend."

➤ Read *The King's Chessboard,* by David Birch (Puffin), and discuss how your child might get the same idea to work for her. (Be careful, she might decide to renegotiate her allowance!)

➤ Do you know what a googol is? It is 10^{100}. Show your child how to write numbers as exponents, beginning with 100 (10^2) and moving on up into the big guys. For example, ten to the ninth power, or 10^9, is $10 \times 10 \times 10 \times 10 \times 10 \times 10 \times 10 \times 10 \times 10$ or 1,000,000,000 (one billion). Look up the names of other large numbers, such as quindecillion or centillion (most dictionaries and encyclopedias have tables of numbers in them) and find out how to write them in exponential form.

HAVE MORE TIME?

➤ Make several copies of the fraction strips on page 220. Invite your child to use the strips to compare and add unlike fractions such as ¾ and ⅔, and mixed numbers such as 1⅚ and 2¾.

➤ Use the language of ratio and proportion. A *ratio* is nothing more than a comparison. A *proportion* is a statement of equality between two ratios.

For example, to cook rice, you might use a ratio of one cup rice to three cups water (usually written as 1:3 or 1/3). If you want to cook twice as much rice, you might form the proportion 1/3 = 2/6 and find that you now need six cups of water. Ratios are handy when dealing with problems of scale (1 inch/1 mile), probability (2/3 odds), and geometry.

➤Show your child how to determine the area of a triangle. Have him draw a triangle on graph paper. Then demonstrate how to draw a rectangle around the triangle. Ask him to compare the number of spaces within the triangle to those in the entire rectangle. What has he learned about determining the area of a triangle? (The area of the triangle is half the area of the rectangle.) Have him experiment to see if his conclusions always work.

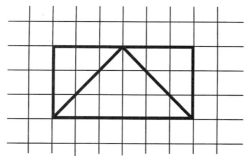

➤Teach your child the mysterious Fibonacci series. Write down the following number pattern and see if you and your child can figure out the rule to the pattern:

1, 1, 2, 3, 5, 8, 13

Give up? Here's a hint. Look at the 2. How is it related to the two numbers before it? Now look at the 5. How is it related to the two numbers before it? What do you think the next number in the series will be?

If you guessed 21, you have probably figured out that each new number in the series is the sum of the two previous numbers. Work together to find the next few numbers (34, 55, 89, 144, 233, 377, 610). The Fibonacci series is filled with all sorts of mysterious patterns. Here are a couple for you to explore with your child. Check the library for books that contain others.

• Add the first, third, and fifth numbers in the series (1 + 2 + 5 = 8). Now add the first, third, fifth, and seventh numbers (1 + 2 + 5 + 13 = 21). See the pattern?

• Add any ten consecutive numbers in the series. Now divide the total by 11. Repeat with a different set of ten consecutive numbers. The total will always be divisible by 11.

➤ Use one-inch-wide strips of notebook paper to investigate these geometric mysteries.

   1. Tape two strips together at the ends. Then cut the loop along the middle, as shown.

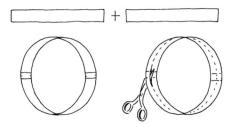

   2. Give one strip a half twist before taping the two strips together at the ends. Then cut the loop along the middle.

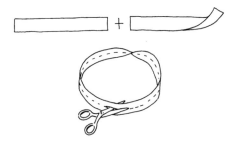

   3. Give one strip a full twist before taping two strips together at the ends. Then cut the loop along the middle.

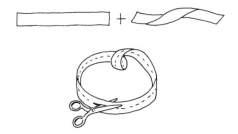

➤ Help your child make a scale drawing of her room. Use the centimeter square paper at the back of the book (you may have to tape a few copies together) and use a scale of 1 cm/1 foot to draw the perimeter of the room. Suggest that your child cut scale-size furniture pieces from construction paper. That way, she will be able to rearrange her bedroom furniture to her heart's content and your back muscles will be saved some wear and tear.

➤ Help your child discover pi (π). Children (and other mathematicians) seem naturally fascinated by this famous number.

1. Trace around a jar lid, bowl, or other circular object.
2. Use a piece of string to measure the circumference (distance around) of the circle. Then measure the circle's diameter.
3. Use a calculator to divide the circumference by the diameter.
4. Follow the same procedure for circles of different sizes. Your child will be amazed to discover that no matter how large or small the circle is, the ratio of its circumference to its diameter is always about 3.14.

According to the *Guinness Book of World Records,* Hiroyuki Goto of Tokyo, Japan, holds the record for memorizing pi to more than 42,195 decimal places. Now *there's* a challenge for a long car trip!

➤ Magazines geared specifically toward the young math puzzler may be hard to find. Look for *Zillions* (*Consumer Reports* children) or *Games Junior* at your newsstand.

➤ If your child delights in numbers, keep an eye out for books that feed that delight. Here are a few suggestions:
- *The Adventures of Penrose the Mathematical Cat,* by Theoni Pappas (Wide World Publishing)
- *Arithmetricks: 50 Easy Ways to Add, Subtract, Multiply and Divide Without a Calculator,* by Edward Julius (John Wiley and Sons)
- *Cool Math,* by Christi Maganzini (Price Stern Sloan)
- *Math Wizardry for Kids,* by Margaret Kenda (Barrons)

Magic square solutions, page 187.

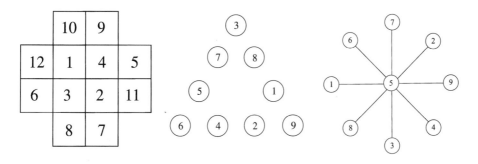

Working with Your Child's Teacher

This book and the accompanying assessment can provide you with lots of information about fourth grade expectations and how your own child is progressing toward meeting those expectations. There is, however, much information about your child's schooling that this book cannot provide.

This book cannot tell you, for example, the methods your child's teacher uses to teach fourth grade skills. Does she teach to the large group, to small groups, or to individuals? Does she encourage children to work together or does she ask them to work alone, or both? The book also cannot tell you the sequence in which the skills will be taught or integrated into the curriculum. Will measurement be introduced in the beginning of the year or at the end? What math skills will be incorporated into a unit on prehistoric life?

Since assessment methods vary greatly from school to school and from classroom to classroom, no book can tell you exactly how your child's performance is being measured and recorded this year Nor can any book give you a clear picture of how your child interacts in the classroom (you might discover that your child can behave quite differently in a different setting) or how your child is doing socially. Both of these factors greatly affect school success.

To gather this kind of information you must form a strong line of communication with your child's teacher. Most schools provide several ways for teachers and parents to share information, but you might discover that you will glean far more information if you take the lead now and then. Here are some ways that you can get a closer look at your child's learning experience.

Open House

Open House, also known as Parents' Night or Back-to-School Night, is an evening set aside for teachers to present their goals, methods of instruction, and routines. The purpose of this event is not to discuss individual students but to introduce the program and classroom procedures as a whole.

Open House presentations are as varied as the personalities of the teachers who give them. Your child's teacher might present you with a brief written description of his expectations, or he might simply invite you to come into the room and look around. He might have you participate in some of the math and reading activities the children do, or he might even prepare a video or a slide show to demonstrate a typical day in fourth grade.

If your child's teacher has not prepared an elaborate or particularly detailed presentation, do remember that not all teachers are extroverts. Many feel far more comfortable in a room with twenty-five rambunctious nine-year-olds than in front of a group of adults. If this is true of your child's teacher, try posing a few encouraging questions to help the teacher provide you and other appreciative parents with more detailed information.

"But," you might say, "what if I am not an extrovert either? And besides, I don't want the teacher to think I'm an overbearing or uncooperative parent!" Indeed, many parents find that they are more anxious on Parents' Night than the teachers are. The parents' own experiences as students or their lingering fear of authority might cause trepidation. After all, whose heart doesn't beat a little faster at the thought of being sent to the principal's office? Simply meeting the person with whom your child will spend over 180 days this year can be unnerving enough to cause you to sit passively at your child's desk.

Keep in mind that *how* you pose your questions can make a difference. Questions need not be challenges. They can be invitations. "What does the study of constellations have to do with spelling?" is a challenge. "Your study of constellations sounds fascinating. Can you tell us more about how you will integrate spelling skills into that study?" on the other hand, is an invitation to discussion. Most teachers are passionate about children and the subjects they teach. Encourage your child's teacher to expound on what excites him most.

Parent Conferences

There are three kinds of parent-teacher conferences: regularly scheduled conferences, special conferences that you initiate, and special conferences that your child's teacher initiates. The purpose of each of these conferences is the same: to discuss how your child is doing and how you can support him emotionally and educationally. Your role in each of these conferences, however, can vary depending upon who initiated the conference.

Scheduled Conferences

Scheduled conferences usually occur once at the beginning of the school year and once later on in the year. Before attending a scheduled conference, you'll want to do some data gathering. Remember, the more information you have going into a conference, the easier the conference will be for everyone. Begin with your child. Long before conference time, you should be asking specific questions. "How's school going?" might not elicit much of a response. However, specific questions, such as those below, might prompt a more meaningful response:

- "What are you working on in math?"
- "What's your favorite thing to do in class? Why?"
- "What do you like best [or least] about language arts?"
- "Does your teacher say anything specific about your writing?"
- "What worries you about school?"

Next, think about learning activities you and your child have done together and any questions the activities have raised. If you have given your child the assessment in this book, you might find that you already have a number of questions. For instance, you might have observed that your child approaches math problems by recalling a procedure: "First I do this. Then I do this." Even if the teacher reports that your child is doing well in math, you might want to discuss whether your child is memorizing ways to solve problems or whether he truly understands the way fractions or decimals work. Tell the teacher what you have observed at home, and see if your observations match the teacher's.

As you prepare the questions you wish to ask your child's teacher, be aware that the teacher herself is preparing to meet with more than twenty sets of parents. It is likely that she has established a routine, such as showing you samples of your child's work or the results of formal and informal assessments. She might have one or two issues she wishes to bring to your attention. Because of the uniformity of these conferences, you might find yourself wondering if the teacher truly knows your child. A comment such as "Your son is such a pleasure to have in class" is nice to hear. But it is not nearly as useful—or, ultimately, as cherished—as "Your son has begun to use puns and figurative language in his writing. He demonstrates a sophisticated use of words." To elicit more specific comments about your child, feel free to ask questions like these:

- "In what areas have you seen the most growth? The least?"
- "How does my child's performance compare with that of other children at this grade level?" Teachers understandably do not like to compare chil-

dren and are often reluctant to answer this question, but it is an important one. Keep in mind that you need to know about your child's progress and performance. The teacher might tell you that your child is growing daily as a reader. However, until you know that the growth that is taking place is in the lowest reading group, you have only half of the picture.

- "What are my child's work habits like?"
- "What are my child's interests?"
- "What motivates my child in school?"
- "Does my child have close and consistent friends? What are they like?"
- "How would you describe my child's attention span?"
- "What can I be doing at home to help support my child's learning?"

If during the conference the teacher uses jargon you're not familiar with or if the teacher describes your child in ways that seem vague, ask for clarification. "A live wire" could mean that your child is bright and curious or that he has difficulty sitting still or paying attention. Try not to leave the conference until you are sure you have a clear picture.

Most routine conferences are scheduled in fifteen- to twenty-minute blocks (which is why you want to be on time for yours). If your conference is coming to an end and you have just unearthed an area of concern, ask to schedule another conference. Most teachers will be happy to do so.

You might find that your child is invited or expected to attend your teacher's conference with you. This format has both its advantages and disadvantages. By attending the conference, your child will be encouraged to take a more active role in his own learning and assessment. You might, however, have questions you would like to discuss with the teacher privately. If your child has been asked to attend, and you do not want to discuss all of your concerns in his presence, request a second conference time or indicate that you will be following up with a phone call.

When You Initiate a Conference

Although you might be tempted to seek information from the teacher during a class field trip or while you're dropping your child off at school after a dentist's appointment, try to refrain from doing so. Impromptu discussions about one child's progress are too much to ask of a teacher who's fully immersed in teaching. Instead, if you have concerns or wish to know more about your child's learning, make an appointment to see the teacher or speak with her on the telephone.

You might also want to schedule a conference or a phone call to inform the teacher of any stresses or special circumstances your child is experiencing. Illness, parental separation or divorce, death of a dear one (including pets), and particular fears can all affect a child's school experience and are well worth revealing to the teacher. It is also appropriate to schedule a conference if you have noticed confusing or unwarranted changes in your child's behavior. You and the teacher might be able to pull together enough information to make sense of the change.

For many children, fourth grade is the year when social concerns begin to move to the forefront. It's easy for a fourth grader to become overly preoccupied with the making and keeping of friendships. A certain amount of turmoil—good days and bad—is normal in the social arena. But if your child is having difficulty with peers, if he is seemingly without friends and longs for them, or if he's being harassed or ostracized on a regular basis, do not hesitate to schedule a time to talk to his teacher. Social acceptance is not an individual problem—it is a community problem. Together, you and your child's teacher can brainstorm appropriate strategies to teach your child and others for optimum success.

At times, your concerns might have less to do with your child's individual progress than with the classroom situation as a whole. Perhaps you take issue with a specific method your child's teacher is using or you would like to see learning addressed in other ways. Parents often hesitate to talk to teachers about these considerations for fear that the teacher will feel attacked and subsequently take her anger out on their child. This common fear is rarely warranted. Teachers know that listening and responding to parents will ultimately bring about more support, not less. In most situations a concern, particularly a first-time concern, is taken quite seriously, especially if your choice of words and tone of voice are cooperative rather than confrontational. In schools, as in other institutions, the squeaky wheel does get the grease. Scheduling a conference and expressing your concern in a genuine spirit of collaboration is appropriate.

If you have a concern about your child and are wondering if you should set up a conference, do so—and do it *now*. (October is not too soon.) It is far better to communicate early when both you and your child's teacher can be proactive rather than reactive. Address the problem *before* your child experiences frustration or a sense of failure. Success is the leading motivator in school achievement. Don't let your child lose that feeling of success.

When the Teacher Initiates a Conference

Suppose you come home from work to find a message on your answering machine: your child's teacher wants to have a conference. Like any parent, you assume the worst. First comes the flood of questions for your child: "How are things going at school? Any problems?" Next comes the steady flow of parental guilt: "What have I failed to do?"

Don't panic. Find out the specific purpose of the meeting. Who knows?

Your child's teacher might simply want to talk to you about a volunteer position in the classroom or about your child's special talents. If she seems reluctant to give you details before a meeting, understand that this is to prevent an immediate and full-range discussion at the time of the phone call. In truth, it is probably more advantageous for everyone involved to wait, process the information, and be prepared at the meeting. To find out the purpose of the meeting, you might say "I know that we don't have time to discuss the issue now, but could you tell me in a few words what the conference will be about?" Then ask who, other than the teacher, will attend the conference. Finally, ask "Is there a helpful way that I can prepare?" This last question will set the right tone, indicating that you are open and eager to work together.

If two parents are involved in your child's education, try to arrange for both of you to attend the conference. This way one parent will not end up trying to communicate information secondhand, and everyone can become involved in a plan of action. Be sure to arrange a means for following up as well. You might want to set up a regular system of communication—sending notes back and forth, perhaps, or calling every Friday. Some teachers even suggest keeping a "dialogue journal" in which the parent and teacher exchange progress reports and observations in a notebook that the child carries to and from school.

Whether you initiate a conference or the teacher does, remember that the main purpose of any conference is to collect and share essential information. More often than not, teachers are relieved when parents bring problems to their attention. You, too, should be glad that a problem has been noticed and addressed. At the very least, by opening a vital line of communication, you and the teacher will clarify important views pertaining to the education of your child.

Student Assessment

When you went to school there were probably two types of assessments: tests and report cards. The same holds true for many schools today. In some schools, primary students do not take tests, except perhaps for the weekly spelling test, but they do get report cards. The report card might have letter grades; it might be a checklist; or it might be an anecdotal report. In still other schools new methods of evaluation called "performance-based testing" or "authentic assessment" use anecdotal records, learning journals, and portfolios as a means of reporting progress. A third type of assessment is the standardized test. Each of these types of assessment looks at learning from one or more angles, and all can be helpful to you and your child—if you understand the benefits and limitations of each form.

Report Cards

Report cards are often considered a conclusion. How well did your child do this quarter? How hard did she try? Many types of report cards, however, raise more questions than they answer. If your child gets grades, you might find yourself wondering what a B really means. Is your child performing slightly above average for the whole class? Or is your child performing slightly above average in her math group? Can a child in the lowest math group get a B? If your child doesn't get traditional letter grades, but receives an O for "outstanding," an S for "satisfactory," and an N for "needs improvement," you might still be left wondering what constitutes an outstanding grade as opposed to a satisfactory grade.

Some schools are moving toward more informative report cards. These usually include a checklist of skills and learning behaviors and are marked according to how often your child exhibits those behaviors (Consistently, Most of the Time, Sometimes, Not Yet). The checklist might also be accompanied by anecdotal records. Remember, the perfect reporting device for all children has yet to be devised. Report cards are designed for parents, so if the reports in your district do not meet your needs, let the principal know.

No matter what type of report card your child receives, try to use it as a springboard rather than as a conclusion. As a springboard, a report card gives you the opportunity to talk with your child. Here are some suggestions:

- Ask your child what she thinks of her progress report. Listen to her feelings and guide her in assessing how well she thinks she's doing.
- First and foremost, praise your child for things done well. In fact, you might want to concentrate only on the positive in your first reaction to a report card.
- If you and your child can see a place that needs improvement, talk about *how* your child could go about improving. Telling her to try harder or giving him incentives (a dollar for every A) are probably not helpful. He cannot improve without a clear understanding of what is expected of her and how she can work on the problem. If you have already pinpointed a need using the assessment in this book, the report card can provide an opportunity to reinforce the good work you have already begun to do together.
- If you have questions about the report card or if you need further clarification, schedule a conference with your child's teacher.

Above all, keep your discussion with your child as upbeat and positive as possible. Remember, report cards can tear down what your child needs most: confidence. So as your child's main coach, review the report card but don't let it define her or give her the impression that your love or respect is based on her ability. Your child is not an A or a C student. She is what we all are, a continuous learner.

Performance-Based Assessment

In many schools, teachers are pushing for changes in assessment. They realize that learning does not just occur at the end of a unit or the end of a marking period. It is happening all the time. In these schools teachers are keeping records while observing children at work. They talk to children about what they know and how they approach problems. In addition, both students and their teachers often save the work that demonstrates learning and keep it in a portfolio.

A portfolio is a collection of work. It might contain several writing samples (usually the rough drafts in addition to the finished product, to show growth), charts and descriptions that show how a child approached a math or science project, drawings or other artwork, and a report or project done over time. Sometimes the teacher chooses what will go into the portfolio, sometimes the child decides, and sometimes they select the work together. In any case, the student is usually asked to do some self-assessment.

Most parents find that portfolios are a good source of information about their child's progress and school expectations. They are able to see the quality of their child's thinking, the effort that was applied, and the outcomes. While reviewing a portfolio, parents and teachers can discuss future goals for the child.

If your child's teacher isn't using a portfolio method, but regularly sends home completed work, you can assemble your own portfolio. Some parents buy artists' portfolios for this purpose; others use accordion files or date the work and keep it in a cardboard box. Study the work in the portfolio for signs of how your child is progressing. Go beyond the teacher's comments at the top of the paper and look instead for changes in your child's work. Praise her for applying new concepts and showing what she knows. As you do the exercises in this book, keep work that demonstrates growth. These might come in handy when you are discussing your child's needs with the teacher.

Standardized Testing

Most fourth graders take part in standardized testing this year, if they haven't done so in the past. Standardized tests are considered "objective" because they are administered in the same manner, with the same directions, to children at the same grade level all across the country. They measure student performance in norms, percentiles, and stanines that allow children to be compared to other children and schools to be compared with other schools. The results of standardized tests can be used, and are used, in a number of different ways. Some of the most common uses are: to determine the strengths and weaknesses of the educational program; to inform teachers and parents about the academic growth of individual students; and to identify children who might have learning problems or who might need a more challenging school experience. (Standardized test scores are often used as the criteria to select children who need additional support at either end of the learning continuum.)

If your child will participate in standardized testing this year, prepare her by briefly discussing the purpose of the test in a low-key manner—". . . to help your teacher decide what to teach next and to help your teacher teach you well"—and by making sure that your child has plenty of sleep the night before the test and a good breakfast on test day. It's in your child's best interest not to put too much emotional weight on the test or the test results. If you are anxious, you will likely convey that anxiety to your child, and any undue tension can hinder test performance.

Most schools that use standardized testing send the results to the students' parents. When you receive your child's scores, read the directions carefully to learn how to interpret them. If you have questions about the different numbers, ask the school principal to explain them. Don't be embarrassed or intimidated. Teachers often get a crash course in deciphering the code each year.

If your school doesn't send the results home, and you would like to know how your child fared, call the principal. If the test booklet becomes part of your child's school records, you are permitted by law to view it.

You might feel that the results accurately reflect what you know about your child. However, if you feel that there is a discrepancy between how your child performs in the classroom and how she performed on the test, speak to your child's teacher. Ask whether the results of the test are consistent with your child's performance. Keep in mind that many circumstances can affect test results. If your child didn't feel well, was unable to concentrate, or incorrectly interpreted the directions, the results will not be valid. If the teacher agrees that the test results are grossly inconsistent, and if the test results affect your child's education (determining reading or math group, for instance), you may request that your child take the test again. Testing companies can and will provide alternative tests.

Standardized tests can be useful to schools, teachers and parents, but they can also be misused. Sometimes this limited—and, yes, flawed—form of measurement is used to determine whether a child should be promoted or retained, whether a child qualifies for special services, whether a teacher is successful, or whether a school system deserves to receive funds. But a standardized test should never be the sole basis of an important educational decision—particularly one that will affect individual children. Observational data and assessment of the child's teacher, parents, and sometimes specialists, should also be considered.

Observing Your Child in the Classroom

Undoubtedly, the best way to collect information about your child's school experience is to observe the class in action. You might want to observe for a crucial hour, a morning, or a full day. With advance notice, most schools welcome parent observers. Send a note to your child's teacher (*not* the principal) first. Explain that you are working with your child at home and would like to learn more about the curriculum and her teaching methods. By watching, you'll be able to help your child in a way that is consistent with what the teacher is doing. Don't be shy about offering to help as well as observe—the more direct contact you have with the children, the better. Keep in mind that not every day is necessarily a good time to observe. The children might be at gym or participating in a special event. Also, most teachers would prefer you not come in September, when classroom routines and rules are just being established. Be aware, as well, that your child might not behave the same way while you are observing as he would if you were not present.

If possible, volunteer to help out in your child's classroom on a regular basis. Being a regular visitor will allow you, your child's teacher, and your child to relax into more normal behavior. Fourth grade is often the year when parents get the message that they are no longer needed or welcome in the classroom. This closed-door policy is neither good for schools nor advantageous for your child. Consistently offer your services and work to build the teacher's trust in your presence.

While in the classroom, take your cues from the teacher and try not to offer suggestions too often. Let the teacher know how much you enjoy being in the classroom. If a concern arises, schedule a conference to talk with the teacher just as you would if you were not working side by side.

Even if you can't come in to school once a week, offer to go along on a field trip or to help out with a special project. As you work with your child's classmates, you will discover a great deal about how children learn at this grade level and you'll learn more about their academic goals. Your child will see firsthand how much you value education. His pride in your participation will go a long way toward helping him succeed in school.

Index

Activity Pages

K-W-L Chart

K	W	L
What I Know	What I Want to Know	What I Learned

Idea Web

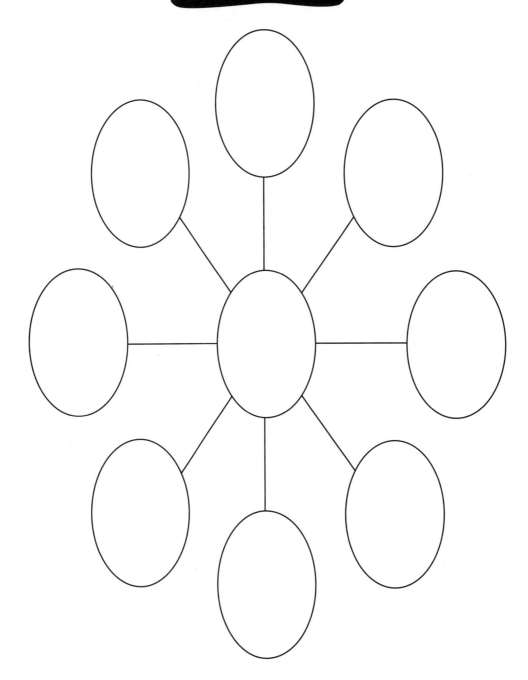

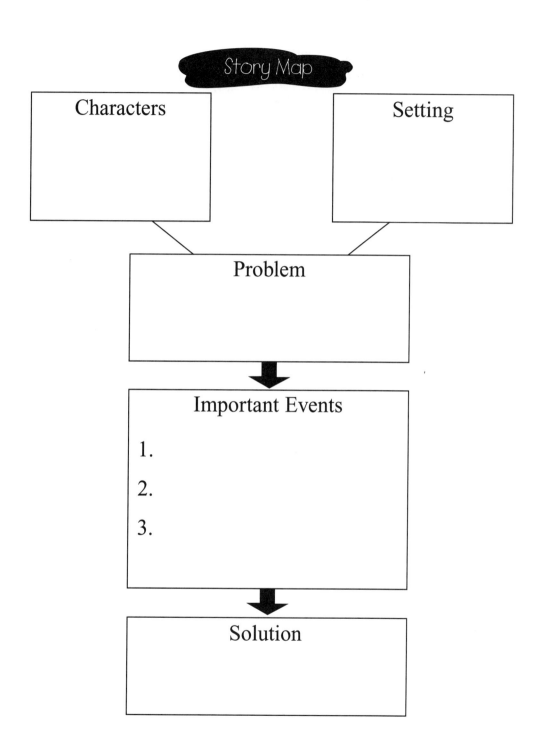

Story Map

Characters

Setting

Problem

Important Events

1.

2.

3.

Solution

Centimeter Square Paper

Product and Quotient Chart

x	1	2	3	4	5	6	7	8	9	10	11	12
1												
2												
3												
4												
5												
6												
7												
8												
9												
10												
11												
12												

Fraction Strips

1

$\dfrac{1}{2}$	$\dfrac{1}{2}$

| $\dfrac{1}{3}$ | $\dfrac{1}{3}$ | $\dfrac{1}{3}$ |

| $\dfrac{1}{4}$ | $\dfrac{1}{4}$ | $\dfrac{1}{4}$ | $\dfrac{1}{4}$ |

| $\dfrac{1}{5}$ | $\dfrac{1}{5}$ | $\dfrac{1}{5}$ | $\dfrac{1}{5}$ | $\dfrac{1}{5}$ |

| $\dfrac{1}{6}$ | $\dfrac{1}{6}$ | $\dfrac{1}{6}$ | $\dfrac{1}{6}$ | $\dfrac{1}{6}$ | $\dfrac{1}{6}$ |

| $\dfrac{1}{8}$ | $\dfrac{1}{8}$ | $\dfrac{1}{8}$ | $\dfrac{1}{8}$ | $\dfrac{1}{8}$ | $\dfrac{1}{8}$ | $\dfrac{1}{8}$ | $\dfrac{1}{8}$ |

| $\dfrac{1}{9}$ | $\dfrac{1}{9}$ | $\dfrac{1}{9}$ | $\dfrac{1}{9}$ | $\dfrac{1}{9}$ | $\dfrac{1}{9}$ | $\dfrac{1}{9}$ | $\dfrac{1}{9}$ | $\dfrac{1}{9}$ |

| $\dfrac{1}{10}$ | $\dfrac{1}{10}$ | $\dfrac{1}{10}$ | $\dfrac{1}{10}$ | $\dfrac{1}{10}$ | $\dfrac{1}{10}$ | $\dfrac{1}{10}$ | $\dfrac{1}{10}$ | $\dfrac{1}{10}$ | $\dfrac{1}{10}$ |

| $\dfrac{1}{12}$ | $\dfrac{1}{12}$ | $\dfrac{1}{12}$ | $\dfrac{1}{12}$ | $\dfrac{1}{12}$ | $\dfrac{1}{12}$ | $\dfrac{1}{12}$ | $\dfrac{1}{12}$ | $\dfrac{1}{12}$ | $\dfrac{1}{12}$ | $\dfrac{1}{12}$ | $\dfrac{1}{12}$ |

Pattern Blocks, Ruler, Protractor

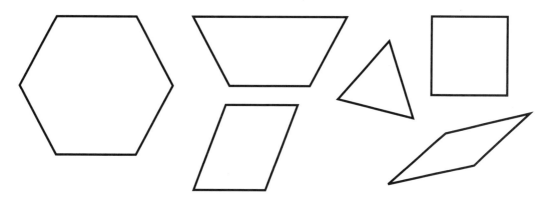

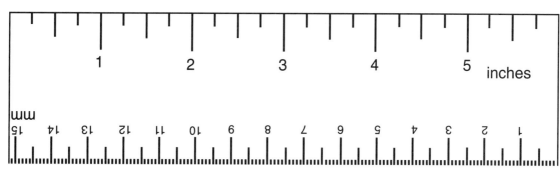

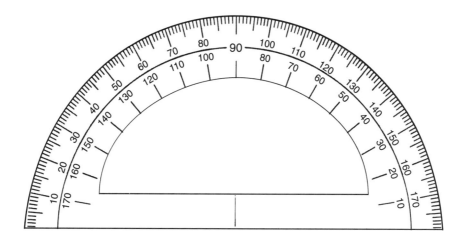